READY, AIM, IMPROVISE!

by Hal Crook

Book II

ADV 14217-02

Book I
ADV 14217-01

advance music

www.advancemusic.com | © 1999/2019 advance music GmbH, Mainz | Printed in Germany

To the Memory of Tom and Pearl Sorafine

Cover Art: 10eg Visual
Layout and music typesetting: T. M. Zentawer
Production: Hans Gruber

ADV 14217-02

ISBN 978-3-95481-066-6
ISMN 979-0-2063-0252-7

 Please visit www.schott-music.com/online-material to download all audio files
for free using the following voucher code: **gcqriBU3**

Special thanks to

Joyce and Zoe Crook, Harold and Ginny Crook,
John and Glenna Ferrara, Clark Terry, Phil Woods,
Bob Brookmeyer, Mick Goodrick, Matt Marvuglio,
Bob Giustini, Ray Bishop, John Young, Paul Ganz,
John E. Sarno, M.D., Hans and Veronika Gruber,
Heinz and Helga Czadek, my teachers and students,
and especially to **IT**.

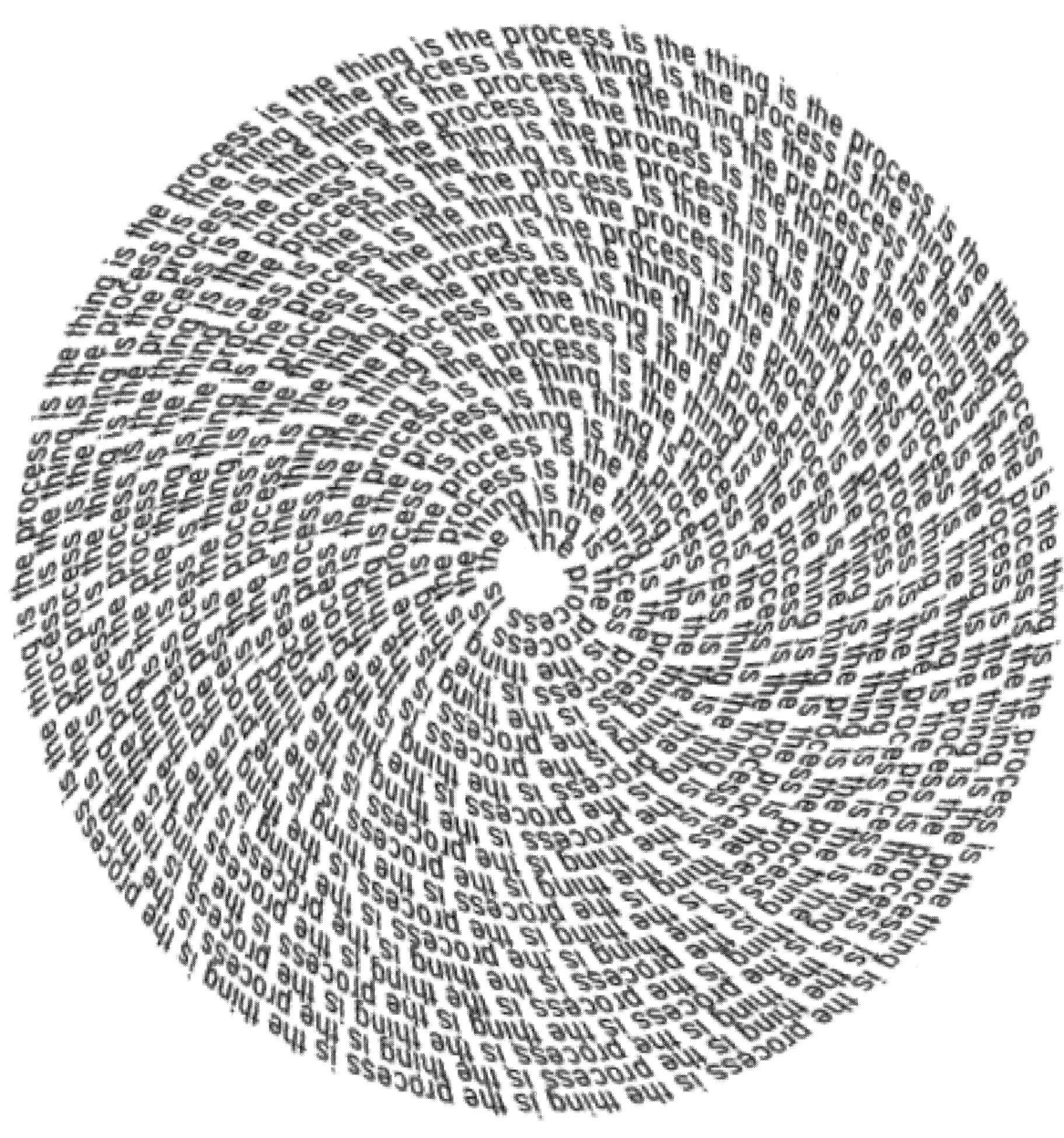

TABLE OF CONTENTS

PART THREE: TARGET PRACTICE

PART FOUR: PRACTICING

APPENDIX

Extra Help: Tune File and Play-Along Tracks

(see p. 8)

AUDIO TRACK INDEX

The audio files are an integral part of this book, which originally came with two CDs. The files can be downloaded on **www.schott-music.com/online-material** using the **voucher code gcqriBU3**. Throughout the book, we refer to the original CD track numbers.

 **1**

Track

1	Tuning note – A concert
2	Tuning note – B♭ concert

**Notes which can be used
for single-note soloing are:**

3	C, D, E, G, A, B
4	D, E, F, G, A, B
5	D, E, G, A, B, (C)
6	A, B, C, D, E
7	B, D, E, F
8	B, D, E, (A, C)
9	G, A, B, D, E, F♯
10	A, B, C, D, E, F♯
11	A, B, D, E, F♯, (G)
12	E, F♯, G, A, B
13	C, D, E, G, A, B
14	F♯, A, B, (E, G)
15	F, G, A, C, D, E
16	G, A, B♭, C, D, E
17	G, A, C, D, E, F
18	D, E, F, G, A
19	E, G, A, B♭
20	E, G, A, (D, F)
21	B♭, C, D, F, G, A
22	C, D, E♭, F, G, A
23	C, D, F, G, A, B♭
24	G, A, B♭, C, D
25	A, C, D, E♭
26	A, C, D, (G, B♭)
27	E♭, F, G, B♭, C, D
28	F, G, A♭, B♭, C, D
29	F, G, B♭, C, D, (E♭)
30	C, D, E♭, F, G
31	D, F, G, A♭
32	D, F, G, (C, E♭)
33	A♭, B♭, C, E♭, F, G
34	B♭, C, D♭, E♭, F, G
35	B♭, C, E♭, F, G, (A♭)
36	F, G, A♭, B♭, C
37	G, B♭, C, D♭
38	G, B♭, C, (F, A♭)

CD 2 **Track**

Author's Notes

Prequisites

The recommended prerequisites for using this text include the following: (1) one or more years of practice on a musical instrument, preferably under the instruction of a private teacher, (2) an ability to read music, (3) a familiarity with early styles of jazz improvisation acquired through listening and/or performing, and (4) information and exercises on various topics from the music textbooks How to Improvise and How to Comp (published by Advance Music), for which this book is recommended as a study guide.

Overview: What You'll Find Where

Following is a brief description of the material covered in **Book I**.

- Part I: Preparation is primarily for beginner and intermediate students but will also benefit advanced improvisers and drummers who need a more complete musical background. The material covered includes: (1) basic music theory, (2) basic harmony, (3) jazz harmony and harmonic analysis, (4) ear training, (5) how jazz improvisation evolved, and (6) methods for studying jazz repertoire.

- Part II: Jazz Vocabulary provides extensive coverage of jazz execution (how to play) and content (what to play) regarding the basic elements of an improvised solo. This information can be used to create original jazz vocabulary as well. Methods are presented for incorporating jazz vocabulary licks in improvised solos. Traditional style jazz improvisation is analyzed regarding execution and content and compared to modern style jazz as a tool for learning.

Following is a brief description of the material covered in **Book II**.

- Part III: Target Practice features a practical, common sense approach to practicing improvisation in which individual aspects of jazz execution and content are targeted (i.e., isolated for practice) using special exercises.

- Part IV: Practicing explores the following areas: (1) organizing a personal daily practice routine, (2) recording your daily practice, (3) critiquing your daily practice, (4) determining your level of musical development, (5) selecting topics and designing exercises appropriate for your level of musical development, (6) assessing your improvement, and (7) balancing your musical experience between private practice sessions, jam sessions and jazz gigs.

 Extra Help contains a tune file comprised of over 300 standard and standard jazz song titles (with a degree of difficulty rating for each song) to be used as a source for: (1) repertoire, and (2) harmonic settings (i.e., chord progressions used for practicing improvisation). Also included is information and musical material relevant to the enclosed play-along recordings in the keys of C, B♭ and E♭.

This part is available online as a free downloadable PDF file for B♭, E♭ and Concert Instruments on **www.schott-music.com/shop/405299**

Preface to the 2nd edition

This second edition of READY, AIM, IMPROVISE! will look different from the first edition in that we have decided to streamline the book's content for the purpose of making it more practical and effective as a guide for learning how to improvise, and to divide the remaining material into two separate volumes: Volume I: Preparation and Jazz Vocabulary; and Volume II: Soloing and Target Practice.

As the subtitle says, the book explores the basics of jazz improvisation. But from utilizing the text in both private and group lessons since it was first published in 1999, I have determined that certain non-technical musical material in the original version leans heavily in an editorial direction, being more or less self-evident in nature, and therefore could be considered non-essential to the main purpose of the book.

By eliminating this material and dividing the remaining material into two volumes – and by offering the formerly included play-along tracks and chord sheets to customers on line for no additional charge – we have presented a more focused finished product, one that still does what it claims to do, but without the distraction of perhaps interesting yet extraneous conjecture. We hope you enjoy the results.

*   *   *

As a professional jazz player and teacher, I get to work with scores of students each year from around the world, all of whom express a serious commitment to studying jazz and learning how to improvise. Many of these students, however, have a limited grasp of traditional vocabulary and its function in contemporary jazz improvisation, while their knowledge and skill in other ares are comparatively advanced. The trouble with this situation, as I hear it, is that when these players improvise it sounds as though they are attempting to *build their musical houses from the roof down*. And, of course, there is a better way.

To me, this indicates that a crucial preparation step in their musical training has either been overlooked, by-passed, or not arrived at yet. It also explains why students do not make steady progress toward their goals, and – in many cases – why the content and execution of their improvised solos are not up to the level of their instrumental technique.

Perhaps there is truth to the assumption that not everyone (who wants to) can or will become a credible jazz soloist. But I have learned that this has less to do with a player's lack of talent for jazz improvisation and more to do with his/her confusion over what and how to practice, and – most importantly – how to recognize and critique the musical details of their playing as they relate to the subject of improvisation.

For just as a painter needs an eye for the details of color, line, shape, and style, a jazz musician needs an ear for the details of melody, harmony, rhythm and execution; or, more to the point, needs to be made keenly aware of the existence of these details and what they sound like in earlier jazz styles, in order to build a musical foundation capable of supporting advanced knowledge and ability *(i.e., the roof of their musical house)*. This is to say that the ability to effectively use traditional jazz vocabulary is necessary to the developing jazz improviser.

The main focus of Ready, Aim, Improvise!, therefore, is to help students understand, acquire and use traditional jazz vocabulary as a basis for learning how to improvise. The explanations, examples and exercises contained in Volume I—together with the extensive information on practicing and self-critiquing contained in Volume II—are intended to satisfy this fundamental prerequisite, and lead to a more advanced study of the art of jazz improvisation.

Hal Crook
February, 2019

Introduction

Words, their pronunciation, and the ways in which they are combined and understood form language. Through language we convey thoughts and feelings and communicate ideas. Hence, we have come to think of any subject involving the communication of thoughts, feelings and/or ideas as a kind of language, e.g., the language of love, the language of mathematics, the language of music, etc.

Music is a language comprised of melody, harmony, rhythm and the various effects created through its execution (or "pronunciation"); hence, a language that is played on an instrument or sung rather than spoken. And, to the extent that music can be considered a language – specifically, improvised music in the jazz idiom – its *words* or vocabulary must consist of the kinds of melodies, harmonies, rhythms and musical effects which make the particular style (e.g., Dixieland, swing, bebop, etc.) sound fundamentally unique. When a new style of jazz develops, then, it does so via extended and embellished elements of vocabulary from earlier styles.

Consequently, when even a capable instrumentalist who is not proficient in traditional jazz vocabulary attempts to improvise in a jazz context, the content and execution of the music sounds foreign, remote, inappropriate, and, in a sense, too original. This is a very different sounding player than the studied, experienced and highly skilled avant-garde jazz artist, whose improvising may still repel some non-discerning ears, but is, nonetheless, permeated with tradition.

Of course, a certain degree of originality – or, rather, musical creativity – is important when improvising in the jazz idiom. But here, especially during the early stages of learning how to improvise, a soloist's search for originality must be balanced and tempered with authenticity and tradition, the all-important springboards for musical growth. Because without familiar sounds and effects (i.e., evidence of traditional jazz vocabulary), even the most devoted listeners and accompanists will eventually lose interest in the improvising, while the novice improviser loses gigs, and, hence, important opportunities to learn and improve.

It simply requires too much energy and effort to appreciate improvising which, at best, sounds inexperienced, untrained, self-indulgent and musically pointless. A soloist who plays so is like a would-be writer who may know the letters of the alphabet but has not yet learned how to use them to form words, and, therefore, cannot communicate through language.

Knowing traditional jazz vocabulary influences the shapes and sounds of a player's more modern and creative improvised ideas, showing an important link between the old and the new, and making the new more accessible, recognizable, indigenous to the idiom, and, as a result, more appealing. It is, in fact, the jazz soloist's job (or basic musical responsibility) to play in such a way that enables listeners who appreciate the style to enjoy the music effortlessly, i.e., without having to work at it. After all, if you appreciate modern jazz, you don't go out and spend $50.00 or more to hear Herbie Hancock play and then have to work at enjoying it! And so it is with all styles; the best improvisers do *all* the work for the listener, whose only reaction should be: *"Wow!"*

For the serious jazz student, then, the ability to use traditional jazz vocabulary effectively in an improvised solo is essential to learning how to improvise authentically in the jazz idiom. The proverbial *break from tradition* that fosters all modern versions of the art form should be viewed, instead, as an *embellishment* or *development of tradition* itself, albeit in some cases an extreme one. So then, by manipulating elements of traditional jazz in certain ways, modern qualities and effects (and, ultimately, modern styles) can be produced.

The music we label today as traditional jazz was, of course, originally heard as modern. Every new form, style or aspect of music begins as modern but emerges out of tradition; and, if it lives long enough, it may become yet another layer of tradition. This cycle – tradition becoming modern becoming tradition, etc. – can be traced all the way back to the first known attempt to create music. But even a modern event of this magnitude almost certainly evolved out of the tradition of speaking or vocalizing; and that, more than likely, from the quasi tradition of random, purposeless sounds; and that, conceivably, from silence.

Tradition implies modern, and modern implies tradition. One contains the seed of the other, and, therefore, they are interconnected; just as up implies down and down implies up; as sound implies silence and silence implies sound. These are mutually dependent polar opposites, since one cannot exist without the other.

Therefore, without tradition there cannot be modern. And the relevant point here for jazz students is that this particular condition applies to each individual player's musical development as well. In other words, *without a traditional background, the average jazz student's potential for becoming a credible modern style player will be severely limited, if not precluded altogether.*

While it is clear that earlier jazz styles (e.g., Dixieland, swing, bebop, etc.) do not need this justification or defense, there are many young players who question the "rule" that one must explore the past to truly understand the present and perhaps create the future. It seems like a reasonable inquiry, too, since it can be quite overwhelming for those students who have only recently begun their study to go back and absorb most or much of the nearly *100 years* of jazz improvisation that has preceded them to date! And while they are busy pursuing that, jazz will no doubt continue to evolve, or at least to absorb contemporary influences, putting the younger newcomers even further from the music of their own period, and making the quantity of work involved to catch up seem utterly undoable.

In spite of this concern, it can also be fascinating and fun to musically probe the past, especially when you understand and accept that it is precisely this activity which – even in moderation – will enable you to progress steadily and perhaps someday make your own bonafide separation from tradition. Remember, though, you cannot break away from something until you are first one with it. This is the meaning of Clark Terry's simple yet profound formula for all aspirants:

• Imitate

• Assimilate

• Innovate.

And in *that* order.

I am not suggesting here that complete musical mastery of each historic style or period of jazz is necessary, but, rather, that a workable knowledge of the basic components (i.e., the melodic, rhythmic and harmonic vocabulary) which make a performance of early and modern jazz styles sound authentic, is.

Consider this: If you were a novice painter but serious about your art, would you *not* spend time studying earlier masters such as Michelangelo, Renoir or Picasso to learn about style, form, content, execution, and how and when these artists themselves expanded or broke away from tradition? The answer seems obvious in this context.

Conversely, there are some students who become permanently fixated on jazz tradition to the exclusion of all other styles and periods. This usually happens because of an individual's intense appreciation or affinity for an earlier style of jazz or a particular player of that style. If this fulfills your musical needs and desires completely and forever, then, of course, it is fine. But if your intention is to explore jazz in order to experience being the best improviser you can be, a permanent and exclusive fixation on tradition will be self-defeating. Although you might work a lot more regularly!

Therefore, if you are a beginner or intermediate level jazz improviser, I suggest that initially, and for a limited period of time, you make acquiring tradition your top priority. Keep abreast of the more recent developments in jazz improvisation as best you can through listening to recordings and live performances, and also by occasionally doing or studying solo transcriptions of contemporary players *who have assimilated the tradition*. Then, after the proper musical foundation is set in place (and your musical house is being built from the floor up versus from the roof down), you can make acquiring tradition a lesser priority, if you so desire. And finally: Be careful not to allow critical opinions about certain styles of music (and about the musicians who play them) to form and take root in your mind prematurely, or before you are musically ready to exclude them as influences. This can prevent you from acquiring experience and obtaining knowledge which you may very well need in order to grow and develop as a jazz player. Don't let biased opinions stunt your musical growth and hold you back, especially regarding the study of jazz tradition.

A vital, natural connection exists between the old and the new in jazz. Recognizing and understanding this musical lineage can help you prioritize your musical goals regarding what to study, when to study it, and for how long. The foremost concern in this area, though, is to know yourself: To give serious consideration to who you are musically, to inquire about what you want to achieve as a jazz musician and what you personally will need from the music of the past to achieve it.

Perhaps the answers will become clear when you realize that, in the final analysis, you simply cannot overlook the jazz tradition and still sound credible as a modern jazz soloist. And, likewise, when the time is right, you cannot avoid the challenging and less traveled path toward innovation and still develop a distinctly personal musical voice.

Part THREE: TARGET PRACTICE

"Failure to hit the bullseye is never
the fault of the target."
                                    – Gilbert Arland

8. Chord-Tone Soloing and Chord-Scale Soloing

Note: For important information on the principles of target practice, see 12. SELF-RECORDING, page 54; and 13. SELF-CRITIQUING – MORE ABOUT ACCURACY AND MUSICALITY, page 58.

For the past few decades or so, more and more jazz players have been using the chord scale approach for soloing over chords in progressions. As I mentioned earlier, the chord-scale approach is based on the idea that if a chord is diatonic to a scale, then that scale can be used as a source to derive melody on that chord. (See 2. HARMONY – HARMONIC ANALYSIS, book I, page 71.)

Using the chord-scale approach gives improvisers (especially less proficient ones) greater melodic and rhythmic mobility (i.e., they can improvise pitch sequences in 8th notes, triplets, sixteenths, etc.). Whereas chord tones must be played in leaps (minor 3rd intervals or wider), a chord scale can be played in steps (major 2nd and minor 2nd intervals), and consecutive steps are much easier to play fast and accurately than consecutive leaps. In general, less experienced players are also more familiar with scales and scale patterns than chord arpeggios from practicing technical exercises in method books, and, therefore, prefer to use chord scales for improvising.

A chord scale contains not only the chord tones of the chord to which it is applied, but also the tensions. Therefore, by improvising on a chord using a chord scale, the soloist will almost certainly play some chord tones and some of the more colorful notes (tensions) as well. It is also likely that without the help of chord scales, a soloist may not know (i.e., be able to hear) specifically which tensions fit the chord tones appropriately in a particular harmonic context.

So, in a sense, chord scales do the work *of* and *for* the ear. They enable an improviser to play active melodic lines which not only agree with the chords but also contain the more colorful melody notes (i.e., notes other than chord tones) which the player may not be able to find or select by ear alone.

However, for beginner and intermediate level players, the chord-scale approach has a potential downside. Many students begin studying chord scales early in their musical education and attempt to apply the knowledge acquired immediately on their instruments. Unfortunately, this often happens too soon in the student's development as an improviser, i.e., before (s)he has learned how to shape (by ear) an appealing improvised melody on a chord or chord progression using only – or mainly – the chord tones.

Chord scales can present too much information, or information which cannot be readily processed, controlled and used musically by the novice improviser. (It is much easier to understand chord-scale theory than it is to apply it with musical results in an improvised solo.) Improvising on chords with chord scales means a soloist can play melody notes which (s)he does not recognize or cannot identify and control by ear. This can result in wandering, shapeless, directionless or mechanical sounding melody lines, often using 8th notes to the exclusion of all other rhythm values – producing undesirable melodic and rhythmic content. Such improvised melodies also tend to outline tonic quality on nontonic functioning chords and vice versa. (See 2: HARMONY – TONIC AND NONTONIC FUNCTIONS: MELODIC CONSIDERATIONS FOR SOLOING, book I, page 47.)

Direction changes in the melodic curve (i.e., the upward and downward movement of the melody line) are also somewhat less frequent because of the faster speed of 8th notes, and less noticeable because of the predominant use of stepwise motion. (Melodic intervals wider than a 2nd or 3rd are less common if not rare in elementary level improvised solos using the chord scale approach.) This produces a melodic curve that is consistently linear, which sounds limited or uninteresting because it is not balanced by more angular melodic curves.

Note: It is relevant to point out here that the pioneers of jazz improvisation relied on their listening/hearing skills and their ability to accurately outline basic chord sound to guide their improvising and to create their inspired melodies. They did not rely on the mechanics of chord scales. Beginning-level improvisers should, therefore, first experience how good it sounds (and how right it feels) to play inside the chords using only the chord tones before experiencing the allure and sophistication of chord scales. Improvising melodies using only the chord tones connects the soloist to the song's harmony, giving him/her a feeling of "oneness" with the music. This feeling of "oneness" with the harmony is essential before a player can hear how to use chord scales and nonharmonic approach notes effectively.

Ideally, melodic ear training for improvisers should begin with chord-tone soloing and then advance to soloing using chord tones with approach notes and/or chord-scale soloing, as shown in the following exercises and examples.

Chord-Tone Soloing

Exercise 1

• (CD 1 and/or 2) – Using chord tones only (roots, 3rds, 5ths, 7ths)

Practice playing the following licks comprised only of chord tones as written in the key of C. Write in appropriate accents, ghost notes, articulation, etc. Exaggerate execution. Then select certain licks to transpose to other keys and practice. Practice writing out your own licks comprised of chord tones only as well. Then select certain ones to transpose to other keys and practice.

Example 177

D–7 or Dø   G7 or G7(♭9)   C or C–   (same chords through #27)

13.

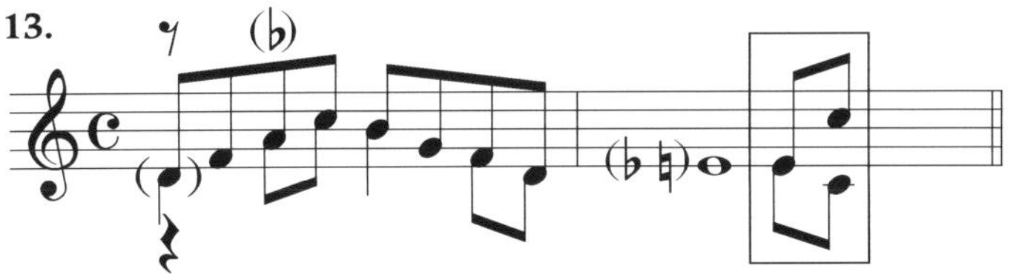

14.

15.

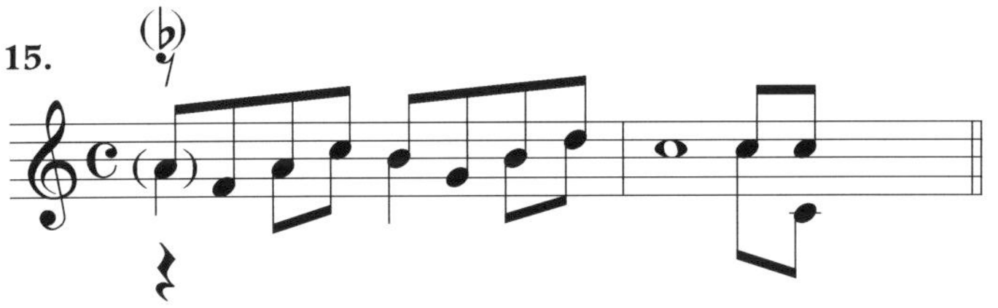

16.

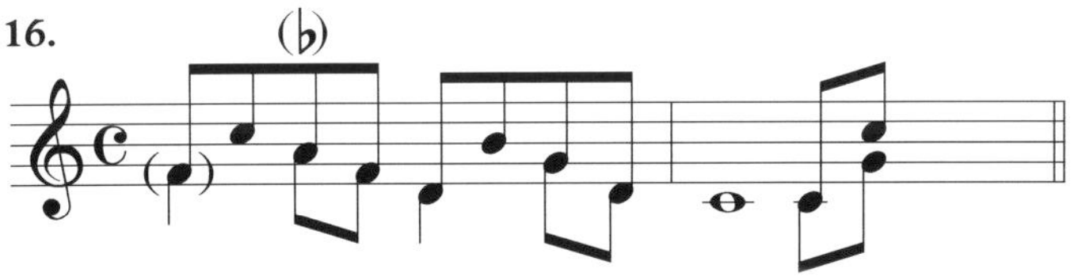

17.

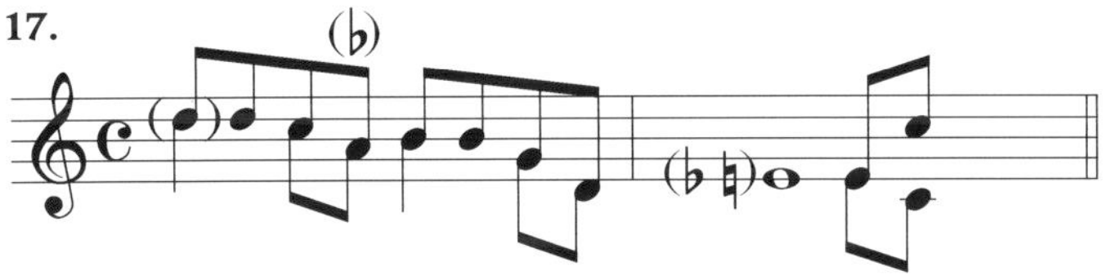

18.

19.

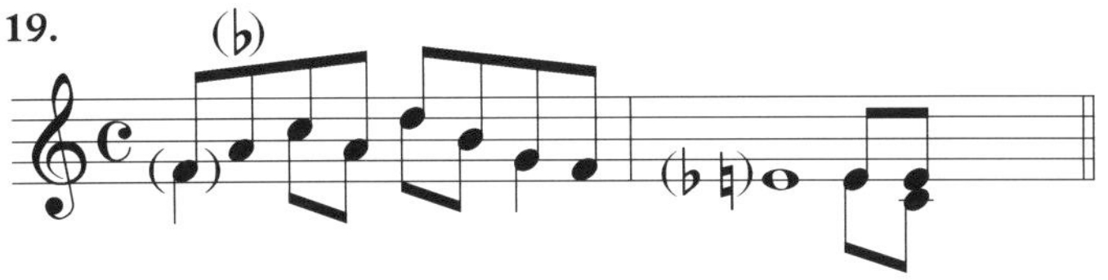

20.

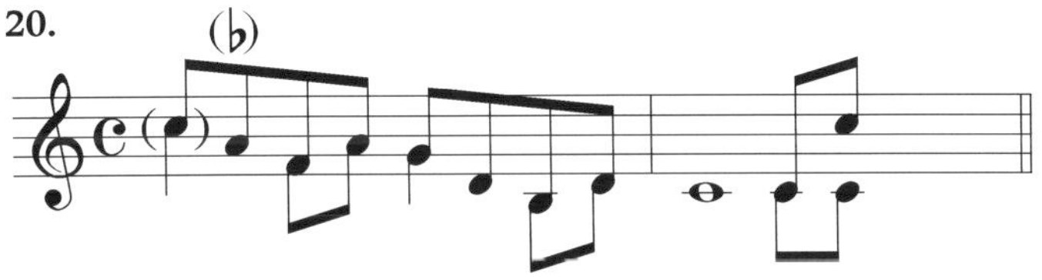

21.

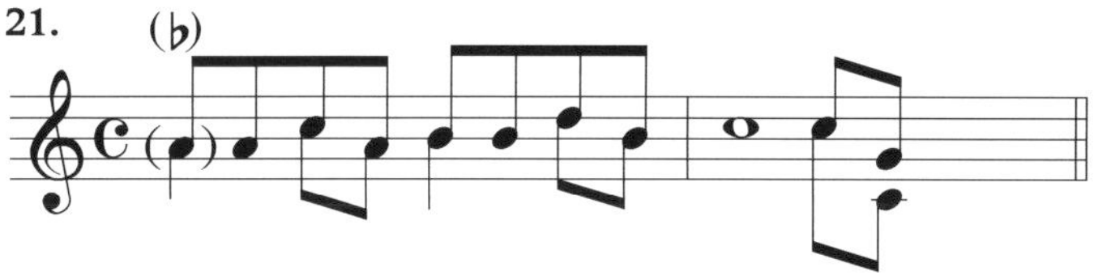

22.

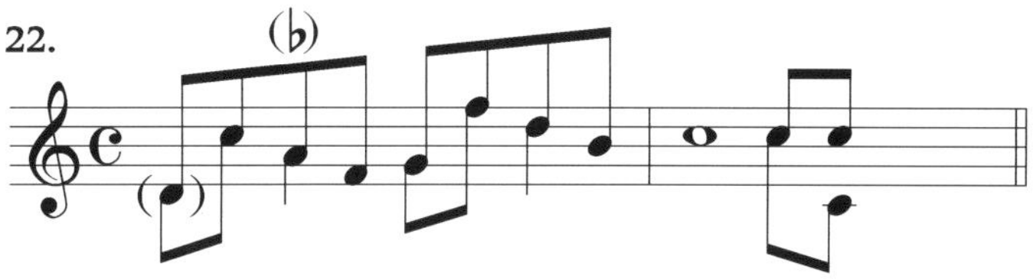

23.

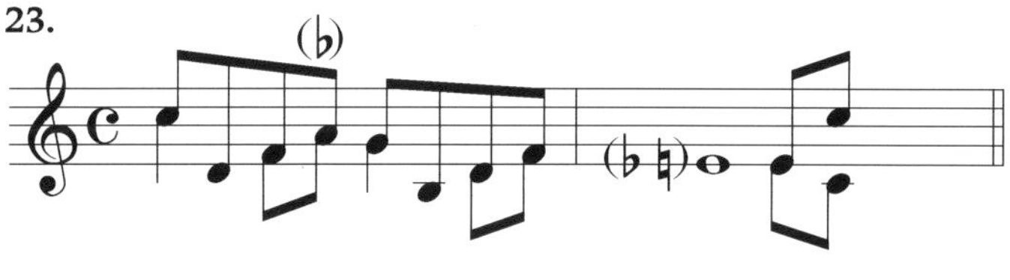

24.

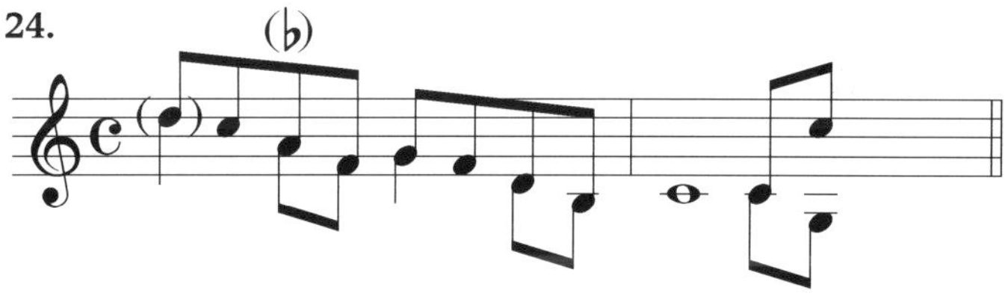

25.

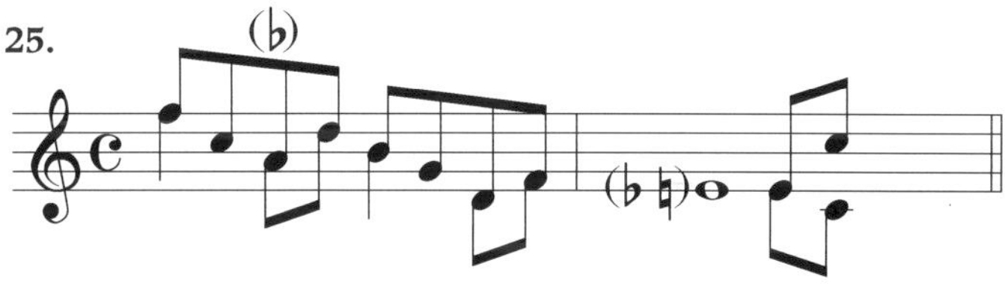

26.

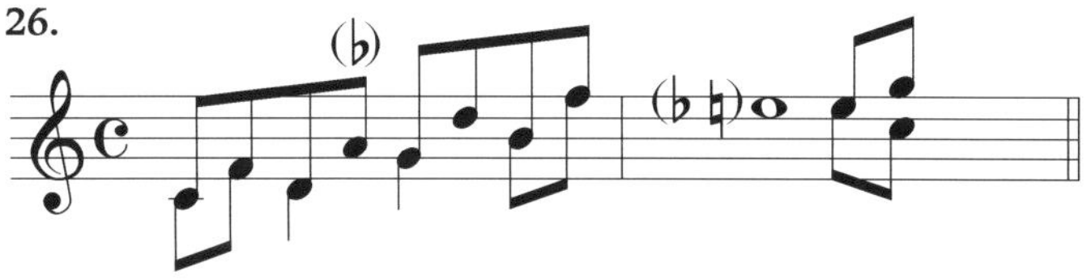

27.

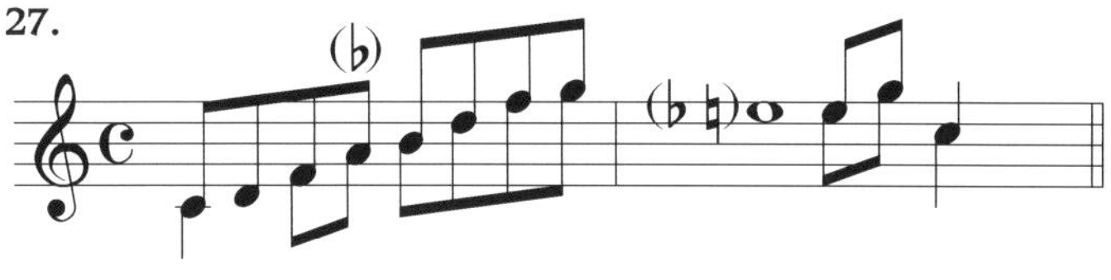

(same chords through #60)

D–7 or Dø   G7 or G7(♭9)

28.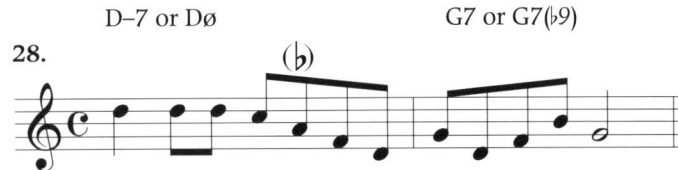

36.

29.

37.

30.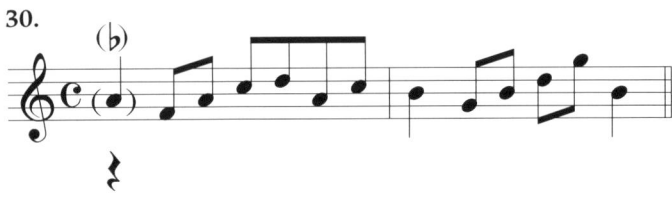

38.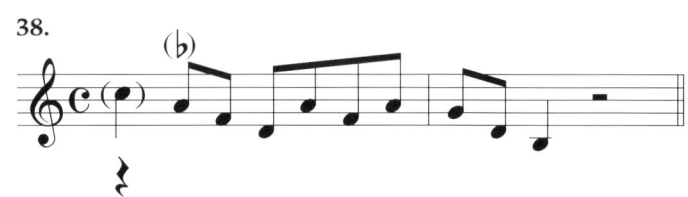

31.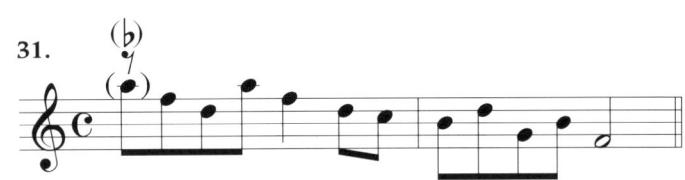

39.

32.

40

33.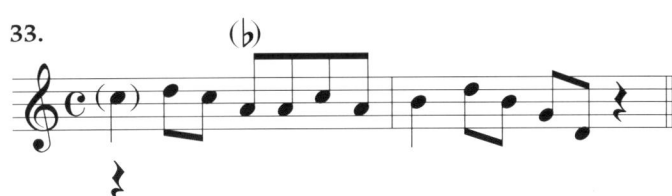

41.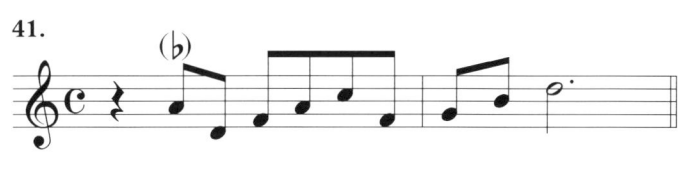

34.

42.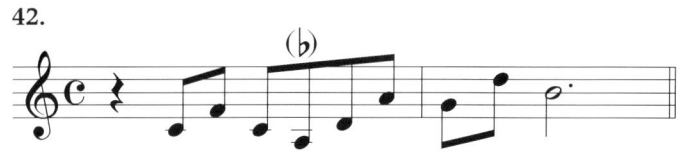

35.

43.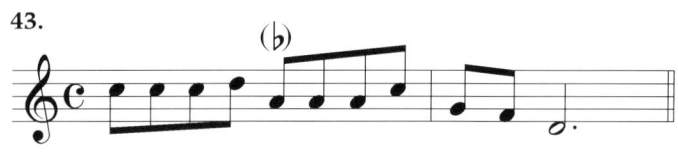

• Record and critique your practice daily.

Exercise 2

♦ 1 Song, 12 Keys, Chord-Tone Soloing.

Preparation

Select an easy standard song (e.g., September Song). Using 12 separate sheets of manuscript paper, write out the song's chord progression above the staff in 12 keys and make two photo copies of each key. On one copy of the chord progression *in each key*, write out the song's melody on the staff beneath the chords. On another copy *in each key*, write out the chord tones (root, 3rd, 5th and 7th) of each chord in root position on the staff beneath the chord symbols to observe while soloing. On the remaining original copy of the chord progression *in each key*, select and write out a half-step connection at each point of chord change (if available) using only the chord tones – to observe and aim for while improvising.

Important

See ahead to examples on pages 38-29 (CHORD-SCALE SOLOING) and use the rhythm motives in groups A thru F for chord-tone soloing also, as follows:

1. Use non-syncopated rhythm motives first (i.e., select from rhythm motives in groups A, B and C, in the examples on page 28).

2. Use syncopated rhythm motives next (i.e., select from rhythm motives in groups D, E and F on page 28).

3. Use combinations of non-syncopated and syncopated rhythm motives.

4. Improvise the melodic rhythm (rhythm of melody) instead of using rhythm motives, while featuring a balance of syncopation and no syncopation.

Note: A good balance to strive for here would be to play a few to several syncopated attacks (i.e., up beat attacks followed by a rest or sustained over the beat line) for every two or three measures of otherwise non-syncopated rhythms.

Practice

♦ **Modal Style**

After memorizing the song's melody and chord sequence in the original key, improvise in tempo on each chord in the song's chord progression separately (i.e., modal style, unlimited duration) using chord tones only (i.e., root, 3rd, 5th, 7th) and a single rhythm motive from each group (A-F) per chord, as shown in the examples on pages 28-29 and as explained above (steps 1-4). Select different rhythm motives to use for each new chord.

To develop a more interesting melodic curve, one exercise could focus on playing numerous wide interval leaps (perfect 5ths or greater) in the melody. Another exercise could focus on making frequent direction changes (two or more per measure) in the melody, while another could target intentional repeated notes (two to five attacks) in the melody. Yet another may focus on combining wide interval leaps with frequent direction changes and repeated notes, etc.

Remember to also *improvise* the melodic rhythm (rhythm of melody) instead of using rhythm motives, while featuring a balance of syncopation and no syncopation.

• Chord Groupings

After improvising on each chord in the chord progression separately, improvise in tempo on isolated two-chord, three-chord or four-chord groupings from the chord progression separately (with and without expanded chord durations). Use chord tones only and a single-rhythm motive from each group (A-F) for each chord grouping, as shown in the examples on pages 28-29 and as explained above (steps 1-4). Select different rhythm motives to use for each new chord grouping. Feature wide interval leaps (perfect 5ths or greater) in the melody with frequent direction changes (two or more per measure) and intentional repeated notes (two to five attacks), etc.

Play all of the chord tones of each chord you play on at first, then use some or all of the chord tones of each chord. Connect adjacent chords melodically by 1/2 step whenever possible at first, then include connecting chords by leap. Play in phrases separated by rest at first, then practice playing with no rest.

Remember to also *improvise* the melodic rhythm (rhythm of melody) instead of using rhythm motives, while featuring a balance of syncopation and no syncopation.

• Tune Progressions

After improvising on various isolated chord groupings from the song's chord progression separately, improvise in tempo on the entire chord progression using chord tones only and a single rhythm motive at a time from each group (A-F), as shown in the examples on pages 28-29 and as explained above (steps 1-4). Feature wide interval leaps (perfect 5ths or greater) in the melody with frequent direction changes (two or more per measure) and intentional repeated notes (two to five attacks), etc.

Play all of the chord tones of each chord you play on at first, then use some or all of the chord tones of each chord. Connect adjacent chords melodically by 1/2 step whenever possible at first, then include connecting chords by leap. Play in phrases separated by rest at first, then practice playing with no rest.

Remember to also *improvise* the melodic rhythm (rhythm of melody) instead of using rhythm motives, while featuring a balance of syncopation and no syncopation.

(See HOW TO IMPROVISE: CHORD-TONE SOLOING, for additional exercises.)

• 12 Weeks, 12 Keys

After one or two weeks of practicing chord-tone solos on the song's chord progression in the original key, repeat the practice in a different key (using chord tones only) for the next week, then change to another key for the next week, etc.

Note: After the first key is learned, do not continue to practice a single key for longer than seven days. Proceed to the next key after seven consecutive days of practice regardless of how much improvement you have made in the previous key.

Continue this process until you have practiced the song's melody and improvised on the song's chord progression (using only the chord tones) for a week in all 12 keys (i.e., for 12 weeks, or approximately three months). Use the following key order or create your own: Start with the song's original key, then proceed through the keys of C, F, G, Bb, Eb, Ab, D, A, Db, E, B, F♯ (Gb).

Chord-tone solo on a familiar standard:

Example 178

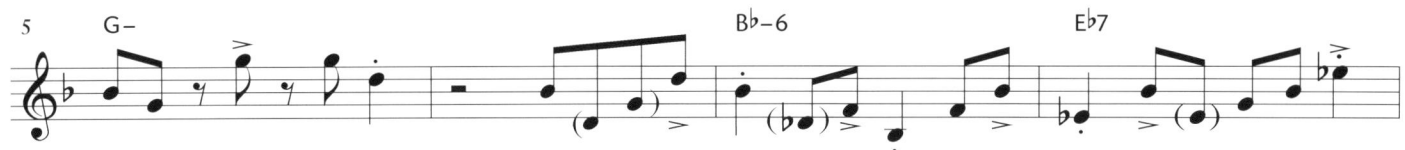

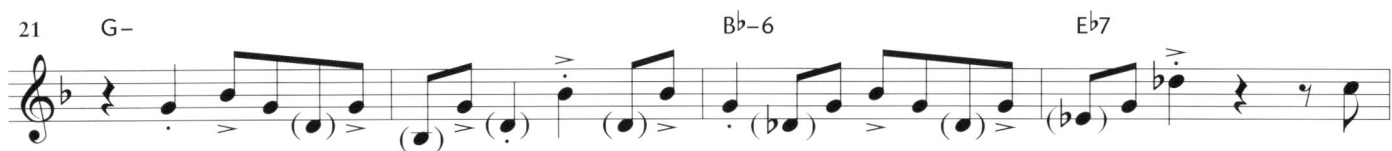

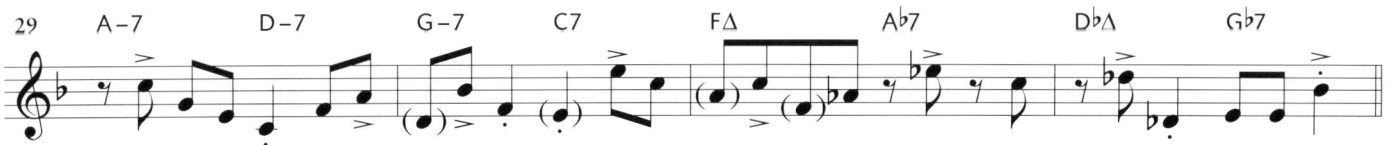

Continued chord-tone solo, 2nd chorus features wider intervals:

• Record and critique your practice daily.

Chord-Scale Soloing

Exercise 1

- (CD 1 and/or 2) – Using chord scales (i.e., chord tones, tensions and non-harmonic notes)

  Practice playing the following licks comprised of chord scales as written in the key of C. Write in appropriate accents, ghost notes, articulation, etc. Exaggerate execution. Then select certain licks to transpose to other keys and practice. Practice writing out your own licks comprised of chord scales as well. Then select certain ones to transpose to other keys and practice.

Example 179

D–7 or Dø G7 or G7(♭9) (same chords throughout)

1.
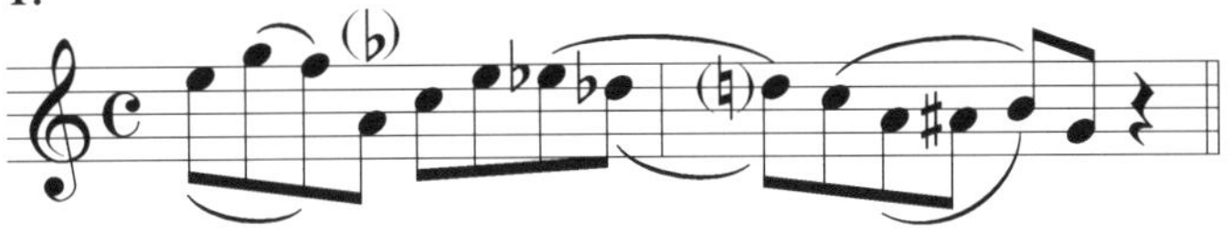

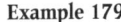

2.
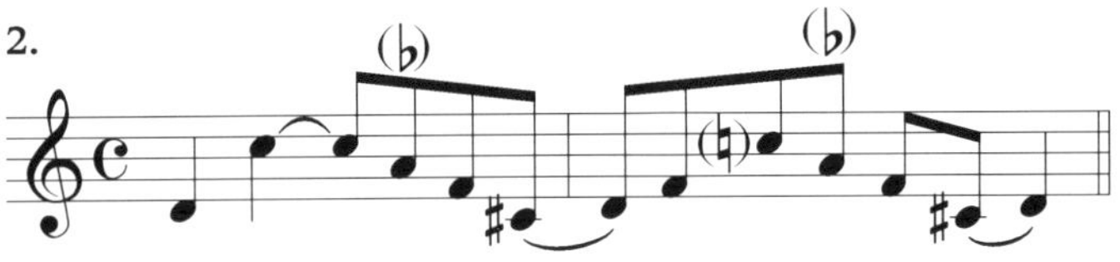

3.
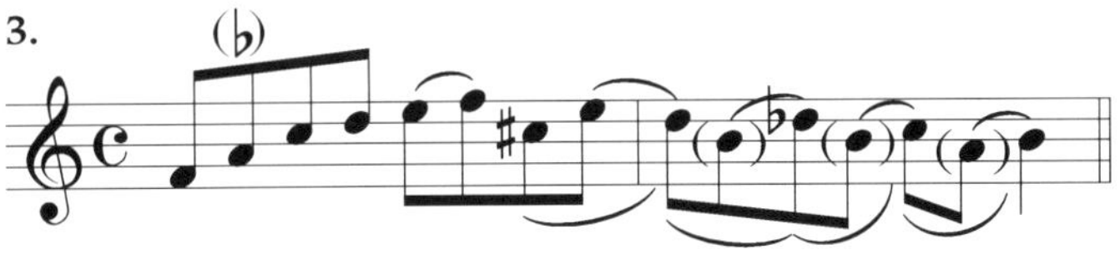

4.
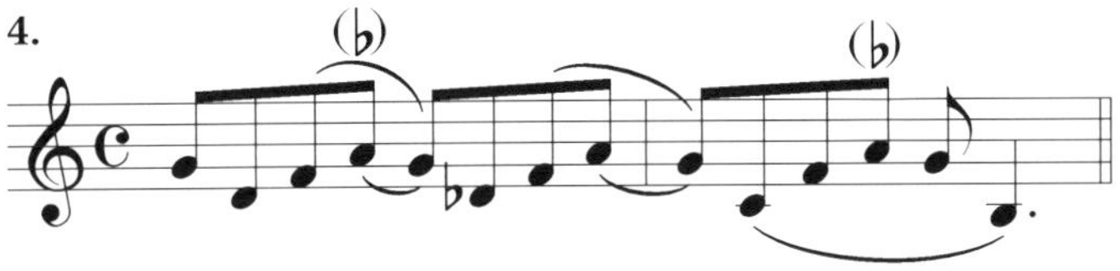

5.
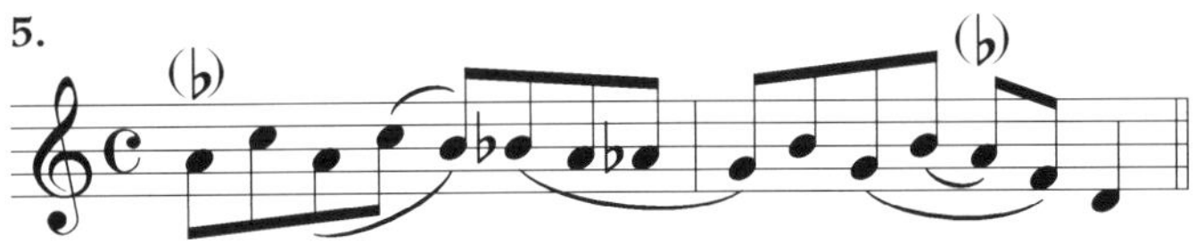

6.
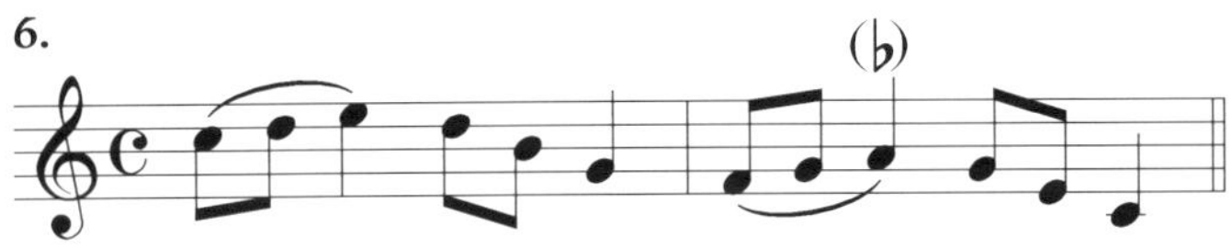

7.
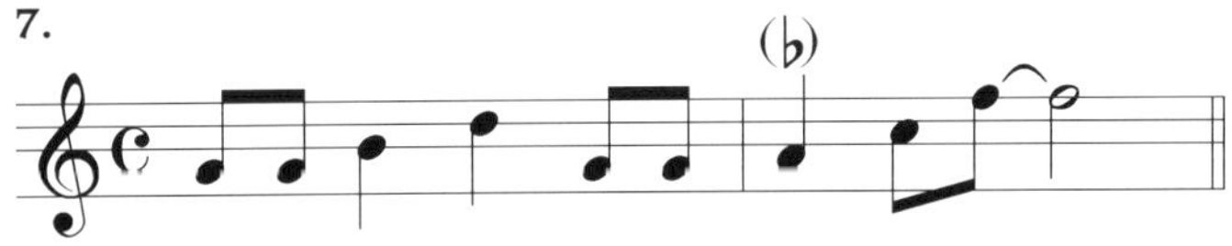

8.
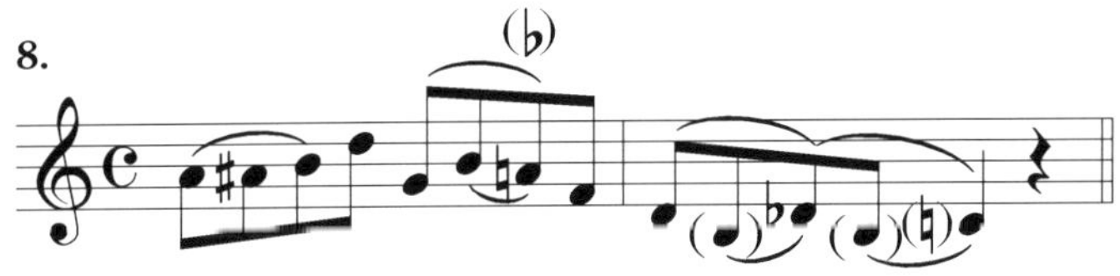

9.
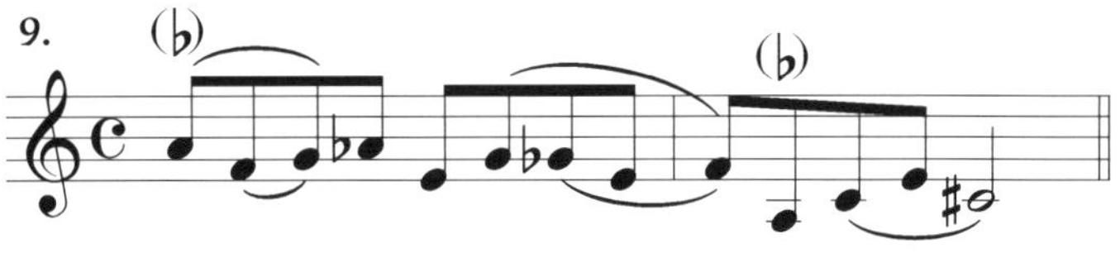

10.
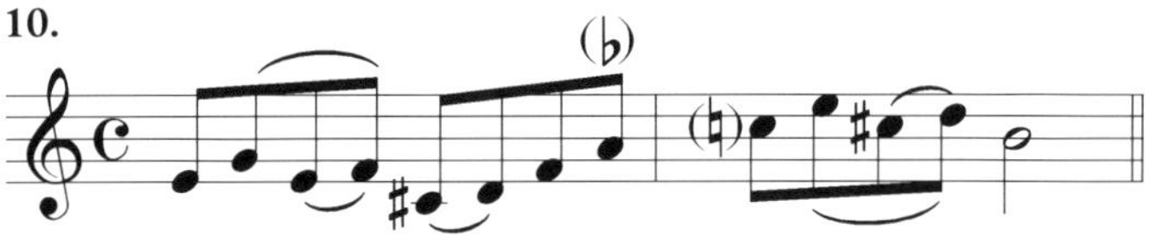

11.
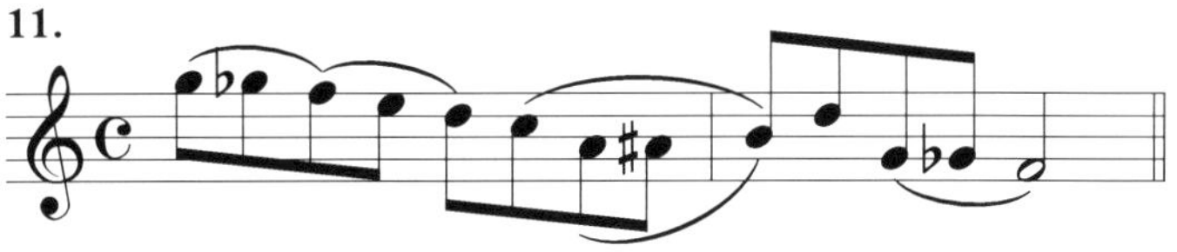

12.
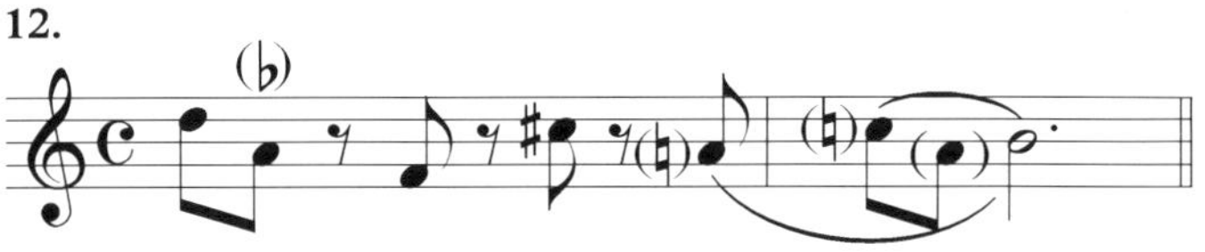

13.
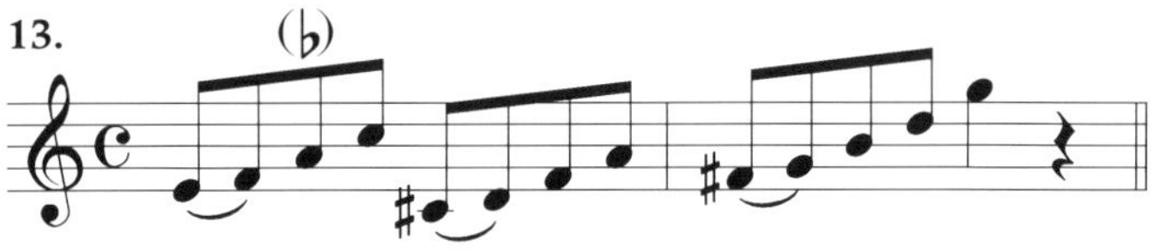

14.
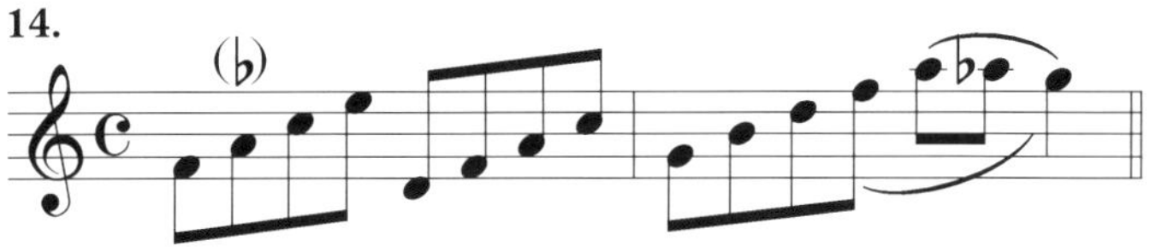

15.
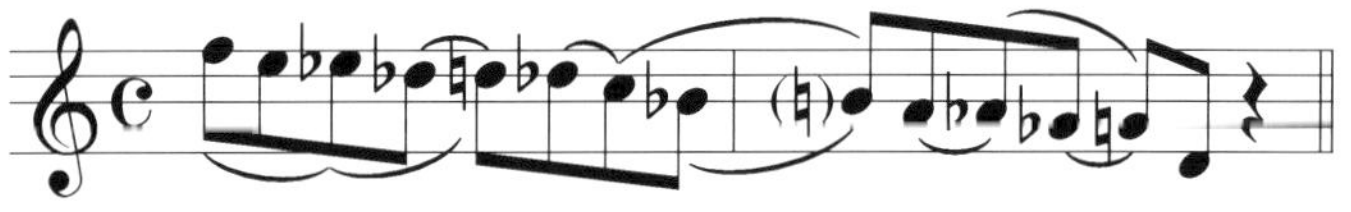

16.
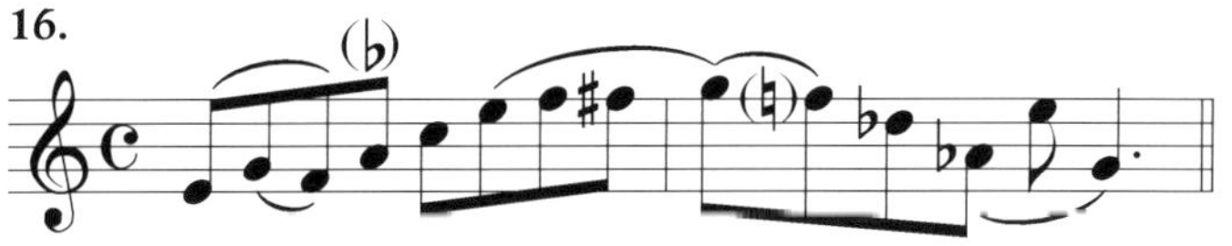

Exercise 2

● 1 Song, 12 Keys, Chord-Scale Soloing

Preparation

Select an easy standard song (e.g., September Song). Using 12 separate sheets of manuscript paper, write out the song's chord progression above the staff in 12 keys and make one photo copy of each key. On one copy of the chord progression *in each key*, write out the song's melody on the staff beneath the chords (unless you are using the same song that you used for chord-tone soloing). On one copy of the song's chord progression *in the original key only*, analyze the chord progression using Roman numerals and assign an appropriate chord scale for each chord. (For help see 2. HARMONY – HARMONIC ANALYSIS, book I, page 71. Also see HOW TO IMPROVISE: CHORD-SCALE SUMMARY CHART and CHORD-SCALE APPLICATION BY HARMONIC FUNCTION.) On the remaining copy of the chord progression *in each key*, write out the assigned chord scale for each chord in the staff beneath the corresponding chord symbol to observe while soloing. (Use open notes for chord tones, use closed notes for tensions.)

Practice

● **Modal Style**

After memorizing the song's melody and chord sequence in the original key, improvise in tempo on each chord in the song's chord progression separately (i.e., modal style, unlimited duration) using diatonic scale notes only and a single rhythm motive per chord from group C (i.e., seven attacks per measure) as shown in the examples on page 28. Select a different rhythm motive from group C to use with each new chord scale.

Begin playing in each measure on any diatonic scale degree (practice starting on different degrees of the scale, covering all degrees); move in one direction only per measure (ascending or descending), cover both directions during practice; use stepwise motion only.

To develop a more interesting melodic curve, the exercise could focus on combining numerous wide interval leaps (perfect 5ths or greater) with stepwise motion in the melody. Another exercise could focus on making frequent direction changes (two or more per measure) in the melody, while another could target intentional repeated notes (two to five attacks) in the melody. Yet another may focus on combining wide interval leaps with stepwise motion, repeated notes and frequent direction changes.

Remember to also *improvise* the melodic rhythm (rhythm of melody) instead of using rhythm motives, while featuring a balance of syncopation and no syncopation.

● **Chord Groupings**

After improvising on each chord in the chord progression separately, improvise in tempo on isolated two-chord, three-chord or four-chord groupings from the chord progression separately (with and without expanded chord durations). Use diatonic scale notes only and a single rhythm motive from group C for each chord grouping, as shown in the examples on page 28. Select a different rhythm motive from group C to use with each new chord grouping.

Begin playing in each measure on any diatonic scale degree (practice starting on different degrees of the scale, covering all degrees); move in one direction only per measure (ascending or descending), cover both directions during practice; use stepwise motion only.

Note: When two (or more) different chord scales occur in one measure, the melody line should move by step in the same direction at the point of chord change to a diatonic note in the new chord scale and proceed by step (in the same direction) through the new chord scale.

To develop a more interesting melodic curve, feature wide interval leaps (perfect 5ths or greater) in the melody with frequent direction changes (two or more per measure) and intentional repeated notes (two to five attacks), etc.

Remember to also *improvise* the melodic rhythm (rhythm of melody) instead of using rhythm motives, while featuring a balance of syncopation and no syncopation.

♦ Tune Progressions

After improvising on various isolated chord groupings from the song's chord progression separately, improvise in tempo on the entire chord progression using diatonic scale notes only and a single rhythm motive from group C, as shown in the examples on page 28. Select a different rhythm motive from group C to use for each successive chorus of soloing.

Begin playing in each measure on any diatonic scale degree; move in one direction only per measure (ascending or descending), cover both directions during practice; use stepwise motion only.

Remember to also *improvise* the melodic rhythm (rhythm of melody) instead of using rhythm motives, while featuring a balance of syncopation and no syncopation.

♦ Other Possibilities for Tune Progressions

Another effective approach on a tune progression is to begin playing in each measure on the same predetermined degree of the chord scale (such as the root, or the 3rd, or the 5th, or the 9th, etc.) and move in a predetermined direction (either ascending or descending) using stepwise motion. Exercise examples are as follows: Ascend the chord scale from the 5th degree in each measure; or, descend the chord scale from the 7th degree in each measure. Another possible exercise would be to ascend the chord scale from the (X) degree in all the odd numbered measures (i.e., measures 1, 3, 5, 7, etc.), and descend the chord scale from the (Y) degree in all the even numbered measures, etc.

To develop a more interesting melodic curve, feature wide interval leaps (perfect 5ths or greater) in the melody with frequent direction changes (two or more per measure) and intentional repeated notes (two to five attacks), etc.

After improvising on the entire chord progression using diatonic scale notes only and various rhythm motives from group C, select rhythm motives from all other groups as well (i.e., groups A, B, D, E and F) to use with diatonic chord scale notes only. With these rhythm motives, do not restrict the melody to stepwise motion. Instead, feature wide interval leaps (perfect 5ths or greater) in the melody with frequent direction changes (two or more per measure) and intentional repeated notes (two to five attacks), etc.

Note: You may elect to first apply this practice to individual chords and chord groupings before applying it to the entire tune progression.

After improvising on the entire chord progression using diatonic scale notes only and various rhythm motives from groups A-F, improvise the melodic rhythm (rhythm of the melody) instead of using rhythm motives, while featuring a balance of syncopation and no syncopation. Remember: A good balance to strive for here would be to play a few to several syncopated attacks (i.e., up beat attacks followed by a rest or sustained over the beat line) for every two or three measures of otherwise non-syncopated rhythms (i.e., downbeat quarter notes and non-syncopated eighth notes).

With the exercise above, it is good to practice playing as many different scale tones as possible on each chord scale you play on at first. Also, practice connecting adjacent chords melodically by 1/2 step at first, and later by wide interval leaps. Play in phrases separated by rest at first, then practice playing with no rest.

Remember: With chord-scale soloing, each chord (diatonic and non-diatonic) should be clearly identified by the sound of your melody line alone, i.e., without relying on the harmonic accompaniment.

(See How to Improvise: Chord-Scale Practice, pages 57-60, and Chord Scales with Nonharmonic Tones for more exercises.)

Important

Certain chord scale exercises listed above under Modal Style, Chord Groupings and Tune Progressions can also be practiced by using non-diatonic (i.e., nonharmonic) tones as approach notes and resolving them by 1/2 step to harmonic scale tones.

• 12 Weeks, 12 Keys (Chord Scales)

After one or two weeks of practicing chord-scale solos on the song's chord progression in the original key, repeat the practice in a different key (using diatonic scale tones only) for the next week, then change to another key for the next week, etc.

Note: After the first key is learned, do not continue to practice a single key for longer than seven days. Proceed to the next key after seven consecutive days of practice regardless of how much improvement you have made in the previous key.

Continue this process until you have practiced the song's melody and improvised on the song's chord progression (using only the chord tones) for a week in all 12 keys (i.e., for 12 weeks, or approximately three months). Use the following key order or create your own: Start with the song's original key, then proceed through the keys of C, F, G, B♭, E♭, A♭, D, A, D♭, E, B, F♯ (G♭).

Rhythm Motives

All quarter notes in the examples below should be played with staccato articulation, i.e., short and detached. Play all rhythms with swing feel.

I. Non-syncopated Rhythms

Example 180a

Group A: 5 attacks per measure

Group B: 6 attacks per measure

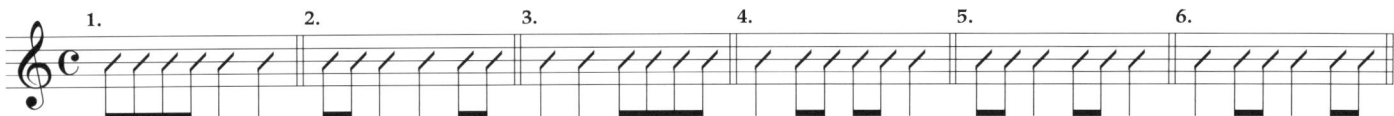

Group C: 7 attacks per measure

II. Syncopated Rhythms

Group D: 5 attacks per measure

Group E: 6 attacks per measure

Group F: 7 attacks per measure

(continued)

III. Combined Rhythms

Combine any non-syncopated rhythm motive from Group A, B or C with any syncopated rhythm motive from Group D, E or F (in any order) to form a two-measure rhythm motive.

B2   **D2**

D2   **B2**

Chord-scale solo (with approach notes) on a familiar standard:

Example 180b

• Record and critique your practice daily.

9. Restriction Means Expansion

Restriction is the core of learning. In sports, for example, restrictions and rules are necessarily used to make the games more challenging and interesting for the players, thereby developing in the players a higher level of performance skill. (Imagine a soccer game played without the restriction of goal tenders, or a baseball game with unlimited strikes for batters, etc; the average performance level of the players would be considerably lower.) Practicing under restrictions, therefore, means increased or expanded abilities for the players of the game, and greater enjoyment for the spectators as well. And, with expanded ability comes greater freedom to be creative and play as you want within the accepted rules.

This principle can also be observed in music. For instance, to learn the C major scale you must restrict the notes played to C, D, E, F, G, A and B; to learn the D–7 chord you must restrict the notes played to D, F, A and C; to play well in a band you must restrict your tempo, intonation and dynamics to that of the group, etc. And then you must practice playing under these restrictions regularly to acquire ability from them.

Restrict Melody, Expand Rhythm

To expand and develop the rhythms used in your improvising, one effective practice approach is to restrict the melody (throughout the solo) to one specific note (or pitch level). In this practice situation, you cannot generate interest in the solo through melody (i.e., with melodic curve, pitch sequences, lyricism, chord tones, tensions, etc.) since there is only one melody note being played. Rhythm, therefore, becomes the main source used or relied upon to create interest in the solo.

Without having to select and play melody notes which fit the chords of the song, you can devote maximum attention to exploring rhythm throughout the solo, and, with daily practice over a period of time, expand your familiarity with the possibilities. In general, players are more inclined to perceive new rhythmic ideas and execute them well when the problem of melodic accuracy is eliminated by restricting the melody to one note. However, you must spend a considerable amount of practice time working on melodic accuracy also before any new rhythmic ideas can be applied in the context of normal melodic soloing.

Single-Note Soloing

The single-note solo approach is extremely helpful to beginner and intermediate level improvisers because it enables them to practice many important aspects of soloing without having to concentrate on playing the "correct" notes as well. These aspects include:

- pacing (play/rest)
- phrase lengths (short, medium, long)
- rhythmic activity (dense/sparse)
- developing rhythm motives (embellishment)
- through-composed rhythm motives (no repetition or development)
- articulation (staccato, legato) and articulation patterns
- accents (downbeat, upbeat) and ghost notes (downbeat, upbeat)
- rhythmic feel (swing, even, double time)
- dynamics (natural, general)

(See 5. EXECUTION, book I, page 85, and 6. CONTENT, book I page 111; also see HOW TO IMPROVISE.)

Important

During the first few minutes or so of our improvised solos, we usually play safely, or only what we know will work well or sound good. This is especially true when we are practicing in a restrictive setting such as a single-note solo. Therefore, in order to create the opportunity to discover and explore new ideas and investigate material at deeper levels, we must practice playing *longer* improvised solos.

For example, if you are accustomed to improvising for one or two minutes per solo (or only one or two times through the song's form), extend your solo length to three minutes, then to four minutes, then five minutes, etc. Work up to eight or ten minute practice solos. At first, do not be too critical of the content or execution of the solo during the extended portion since playing a longer-than-usual solo will be challenging enough.

It is usually necessary to play until you have exhausted what you already know (i.e., your vocabulary) – and do so many times – before you discover something melodically, harmonically or rhythmically new. Once a new sound, rhythm or idea is discovered, it must be played often so that you become comfortable and natural with it. Then, as the material becomes part of your vocabulary of usable sounds, rhythms and ideas, the search for more new material to "improvise" may be resumed.

Remember: Recording and critiquing parts of your daily practice is extremely helpful for discovering new ideas in your solos, and for becoming more aware of the effectiveness (or ineffectiveness) of your old familiar ideas as well. (See 12. SELF-RECORDING, page 54.)

Exercises

1. (CD 1 and/or 2)

   Single-note soloing can be practiced with metronome accompaniment only or with a play-along recording of a standard song progression. The selected single note should be harmonic (or agreeable sounding) to all or most of the chords of the song, e.g., the root or perfect 5th of the song's key signature usually works well on standard songs. Play in phrases (one to three measures long) separated by rest. Define the song's tempo and meter with the rhythms played, then define alternate tempos and/or meters with the rhythms played for special effect. Exaggerate execution while exploring syncopation, polyrhythms, sparse and dense rhythmic activity, etc.

Single-note solo on the chord progression of a familiar standard using the root of the key: G

Note: When practicing this solo, first learn the rhythm only, i.e., without the accents, ghost notes, dynamics, etc. Then practice adding the effects one at a time.

Example 181

2. (CD 1 and/or 2)

   After a period of improvising rhythms using a single note in various settings, use two or three selected pitches in similar settings. The pitches may be selected arbitrarily and played in any octave and in any sequence while considering their interval relationships to the chords of the song.

Three-note solo (root, M2, P5 of key) on the chord progression of a familiar standard (this solo uses the same rhythm as the previous single-note solo):

Example 182

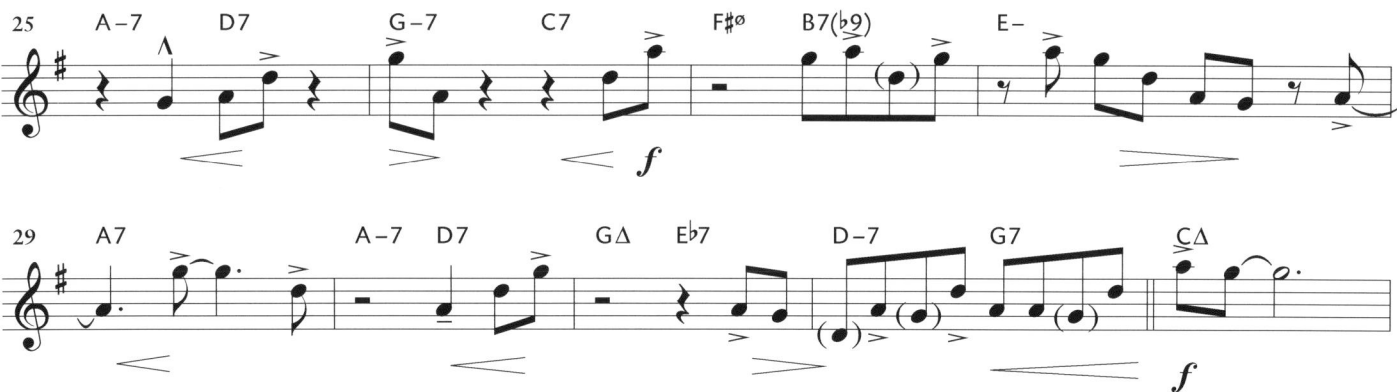

● Record and critique your practice daily.

Restrict Rhythm, Expand Melody

Just as restricting the melodic choices to a single note enables the soloist to develop greater ability to control rhythm, restricting the rhythm of an improvised solo to a single rhythm value (e.g., quarter notes only, or half notes only, or a rhythm motive, etc.) enables the soloist to focus more attention on the selection of melody notes, and thereby develop greater ability to control melody.

The 8th-Note Status Quo

Probably the most often used rhythm value in improvised solos – regardless of the soloist's musical capabilities – is the 8th note. Eighth notes move at twice the speed of the song's tempo which make them more challenging to play than longer note values, especially at medium and fast tempos. Many experienced soloists, however, prefer to play lots of 8th notes and shorter values as well because they (the players) appear to have greater control over the music when it sounds fast. Provided it also sounds good!

But less experienced improvisers – who often feel challenged and compelled to meet the 8th-note status quo – actually need to slow down the rate of speed at which the melody notes change so that they can practice guiding the selection of melody notes by ear. Ironically, playing longer note values can make certain players' melodies sound less accurate and less appealing than if they played 8th notes, which is evidence that their ear is not in control. Shaping and guiding melody lines by ear is unquestionably one of the most basic and important musical abilities that every soloist must develop through practice.

Quarter-Note Soloing *(Give Your Ear a Chance)*

One way to insure that your ear gets this exercise is to slow the tempo down and limit the rhythm values used throughout the solo to quarter notes only or larger values, e.g., dotted quarter notes only, or half notes only, etc. With quarter notes (as compared to 8th notes), you have twice as long to hear and control the selection of the next note in an improvised melody line. With half notes you have four times as long to select the next note compared to 8th notes!

Of course, with quarter notes the extra time only amounts to a fraction of a second per note choice, but the effects are accumulative and, therefore, you will feel less internal pressure to choose a note by ear. Reducing this pressure even slightly creates a more relaxed condition, which, in turn, enables you to not only hear more acutely each melody note being played, but also to hear subsequent melodic possibilities as well. From this exercise, you can actually learn to hear one or more notes *ahead* of the current note you are playing, i.e., to hear not only where you are but also where you want to go. This is obviously a tremendous advantage for improvisers.

For some players, giving their ear extra time to select the next melody note will produce weaker results than usual at first, causing the players to question the validity of the "ear" approach. But this situation only happens to players who have had extremely limited experience guiding their improvising (melodically) by ear. With practice, their doubts will go away and the musical results will improve.

Note: I have noticed on countless occasions that students who feel nervous, anxious or insecure while soloing have greater difficulty allowing their hearing to guide the melody line and other important aspects of soloing than those players who are relaxed and trust their ears to do the job. Therefore, even when the music is loud, fast and intense, the first and foremost goal of an improviser should be to relax – which, it is important to note, cannot be expected to simply happen by itself; you must *practice* relaxed in order to *perform* relaxed. Remember: *As you practice, so do you play.* (See 3. EAR TRAINING, book I, page 73.)

As difficult as it may be to begin selecting and guiding melody notes by ear while you improvise, with practice it will get easier and more natural, especially when larger note values are used to provide more time between melody notes to make a choice.

When the rhythm of an improvised melody line is restricted to a single rhythm value, the player cannot generate enough variety or interest in the solo through rhythm and therefore relies on the other musical elements available, but mainly on melody. Various aspects of execution can also be used to create interest while the rhythm is restricted, including: accents, articulation, dynamics, rhythmic feel, phrase lengths, etc. However, especially when using larger rhythm values, the melody notes themselves (i.e., the pitches) have the most fundamental impact on the music.

When the rhythm of the melody is restricted, it requires no attention from the soloist except for starting and stopping each phrase. Therefore, more energy and concentration can be applied to the melody, resulting (eventually) in more appealing note choices, lyrical phrases, wider intervals, unusually angular melodic curves, colorful nonharmonic tensions (resolved properly), and development of melodic shapes and ideas.

Quarter-note solo on the chord progression of a familiar standard:

Example 183

Exercises

1. **Quarter-Note Soloing** (CD 1 and/or 2)

   Improvise in tempo in a familiar harmonic setting while restricting the rhythm values to quarter notes only. Vary the articulation between staccato and legato at will. With this approach, the melody line is still played in phrases (i.e., with beginnings and endings, followed by rest), but for now the rhythm value of each melody note will be limited to quarter notes only, played on consecutive downbeats or upbeats.

   Playing consecutive *downbeat* quarter-notes in phrases separated by rest will sound similar to an interrupted walking bass line. Phrases may be short (two to four beats), medium or long, and melody notes may be harmonic (agreeable sounding) or nonharmonic (disagreeable sounding) to the chords of the song – provided the nonharmonic notes are either resolved by 1/2 step to harmonic tones (directly or indirectly) or used in sequential melodic patterns (see previous example).

2. **Quarter Notes and Chord Tones** (CD 1 and/or 2)

   Repeat the above exercise but also restrict the melody notes to chord tones only, i.e., roots, 3rds, 5ths and 7ths. This will help you learn to hear and play "inside" the harmony of the song. It is an especially effective combination exercise for beginner level improvisers, or for any player who wants better control over a chord progression (see 8. CHORD-TONE SOLOING, page 14.)

Quarter-note/chord-tone solo on the chord progression of a familiar standard:

Example 184

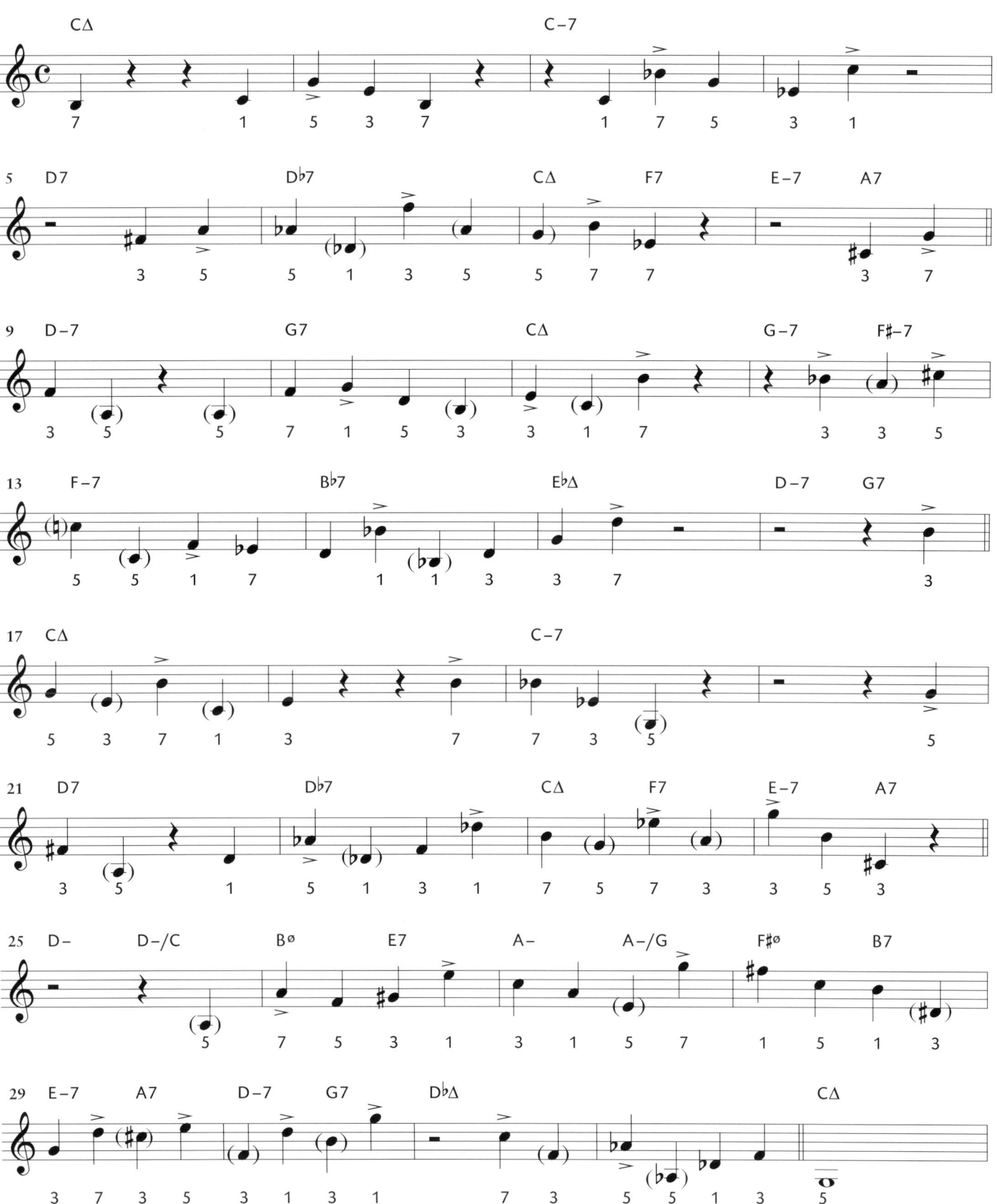

3. **Other Rhythm Values** (CD 1 and/or 2)

Repeat the above exercises but restrict the rhythm to dotted quarter notes only, then to half notes only. Then use *smaller* note values, such as 8th notes only, triplets only, etc.

Note: Because of the greater difficulty of hearing and playing smaller note values, these should be practiced in a very easy and familiar harmonic setting and at a slow tempo.

♦ Record and critique your practice daily.

Restrict Harmony, Expand Melody and Rhythm – Modal Soloing

Modal soloing means improvising on a single (or unchanging) chord for an extended or unlimited duration. Even though a single chord is comprised of only three or four chord tones, various additional harmonic tensions and nonharmonic notes properly resolved can also be incorporated into the melody lines played over the chord. Improvising for several minutes at a time on a single chord, therefore, is an effective way to more thoroughly explore all the melodic possibilities on the chord.

Due to the extended or unlimited duration of each chord in a modal setting, the stress and pressure felt by the improviser to be melodically accurate is greatly reduced. It is for this reason that modal settings are often preferable to use when practicing unfamiliar or challenging topics of improvisation.

Note: Players who are more familiar with improvising on chord changes may find that modal progressions are harmonically limiting and, consequently, boring. These players, however, are relying on constant chord changes to create variety and interest in the solo *because* their ability to improvise interesting melodic lines on a single chord is weak or under-developed. Obviously, this is yet another good reason to practice modal soloing.

With modal improvisation, the soloist can easily devote more attention to exploring the rhythm of the solo as well. In fact, there is a tendency to give special attention to the rhythm of the solo when restricting the harmony to a single chord, because even though all 12 notes of the chromatic scale are available as melody notes on any given chord, the pitch axis (root tone) and tonality (e.g., major 7th, dominant 7th, minor 7th, minor 7♭5, etc.) of the chord remain the same. This means that each individual melody note's relationship to the harmony will be unchanging (i.e., of limited color and interest), and, therefore, the soloist must rely on rhythm (as well as execution) to generate additional interest.

To create accompaniment for single chord soloing, record five or more minutes of each of the chord types listed below in several (or all) keys using root position voicings (root, 3rd, 5th, 7th) sustained in the lower-mid register of the piano keyboard, but without stating a tempo, (i.e., strike a chord on the piano while pressing down the piano's sustain pedal to expand the duration of the chord sound, then attack/sustain the chord again as the sound level decays).

Since a specific tempo is not stated on the recording, a different tempo can be used every day (if so desired) by setting the metronome on a new marking while you improvise with the tape. Or, you can practice improvising rubato (i.e., without defining a consistent tempo). In any case, such accompaniment will provide the basic harmonic background and support needed to hear and study the various melody/harmony relationships available on each chord, while enabling you to explore rhythm as well.

Chord Types for Modal Practice (Record in All Keys for Accompaniment)

• major 7th

• dominant 7th

• augmented dominant 7th

• minor 6th

• minor 7th

• minor 7♭5

• diminished 7th

• augmented major 7th [major 7(♯5)]

Exercises

1. **Ear Training** (CD 1)

   Sustain each note of the chromatic scale on your instrument for several seconds against the recorded chord tones [only] of a selected chord.

   Through this exercise the sound of all possible melody/harmony relationships on a chord can be identified, studied individually and absorbed more completely. Nonharmonic tones can be sustained and then resolved (at will) by 1/2 step to harmonic tones using your ear to guide the resolution. Once you can control the resolutions of nonharmonic tones by ear, these colorful notes can be used more successfully (i.e., lyrically) in improvised melody lines (see 6. CONTENT – MELODY/HARMONY INTERVAL RELATIONSHIPS, book I, page 111, and also HOW TO IMPROVISE: NONHARMONIC MELODY NOTES).

   Repeat the above procedure using a different chord of the same type, or using a different type of chord but with the same root tone.

2. **Modal Soloing** (CD 1)

   Select a single chord and appropriate chord scale. In tempo with chordal accompaniment, improvise in phrases for several minutes on the selected chord using only the notes of the chord scale (i.e., do not use nondiatonic notes for now). Explore various aspects of soloing such as rhythm (syncopation), melodic curve (wide intervals, repeated notes), execution, pacing, etc. (See HOW TO IMPROVISE: CHORD SCALE PRACTICE, pages 57-60 for more exercises.)

3. **Modal Soloing with Passing Tones** (CD 1)

   Select a single chord and appropriate chord scale. In tempo with chordal accompaniment, improvise in phrases for several minutes on the selected chord using notes of the chord scale as well as nondiatonic approach notes (i.e., the chromatic scale). Explore various aspects of soloing. (See 6. CONTENT – APPROACH-NOTE TECHNIQUES, book I, page 120; also see HOW TO IMPROVISE: CHORD SCALES WITH SELECTED NONHARMONIC TONES and CHROMATIC SCALE for more exercises.)

Modal solo on the chord progression of a familiar standard:

Example 185

swing feel

• Record and critique your practice daily.

10. Inside the Outside Chords

Key-Area Harmony

The harmony of a song will often be comprised of chord groupings which establish specific tonal areas or centers (i.e., major or minor keys). Such chord groupings are called *chord patterns* or *key-area progressions* and feature diatonic (or inside-the-key) chords primarily, but may also involve certain nondiatonic (or outside-the-key) chords as well. The nondiatonic chords in this case are usually four beats or less in duration. They generally do not create a modulation to another key, but, instead, move on to diatonic (or otherwise related) chords from the original key, or key of the moment.

Common key-area chord progressions include the following:

Example 186

I Got Rhythm

IΔ	V7/II	II–7	V7
CΔ	A7* (C#o7)	D–7	G7
	(#Io7)		

Lush Life

IΔ	bVII7	IΔ
CΔ	Bb7*	CΔ

Killer Joe

(C7)		(C7)
(I7)		(I7)

Blues

I7	IV7	I7	
C7	F7*	C7	⁒

Blues

I7	I7/3	IV7	#IVo7	I7/5	
C7	C7/E	F7*	F#o7*	C7/G	⁒

Pensativa

IΔ	sV7	IΔ
CΔ	Db7*	CΔ

Well You Needn't

(C7)		(C7)
(I7)		(I7)

* nondiatonic chord

Seven Steps to Heaven

IΔ   ♭VII7   VII7   IΔ

𝄞 𝄴 CΔ | B♭7 *   B7 * | CΔ   ‖

The Song Is You

IΔ   VII7   II–7   V7

𝄞 𝄴 CΔ | B7 * | D–7 | G7   ‖

Night And Day

#IVø   IV–7   III–7   ♭III°7   II–7   V7   IΔ

𝄞 𝄴 ⁹F#ø * | ¹⁰F–7 * | ¹¹E–7 | ¹²E♭°7 * | ¹³D–7 | ¹⁴G7 | ¹⁵CΔ ‖

Someday My Prince Will Come

IΔ   III7   IVΔ

𝄞 𝄴 CΔ | E7(♭9) * | FΔ   ‖

Like Someone In Love
(two beats each chord)

          (V7/VI)   (A–)
                       (VI–)

My Silent Love

IΔ   V7/III   III–

𝄞 𝄴 CΔ | B7(♭9) * | E–   ‖

Easy To Love

IΔ   sV7/III   III–7   V7/II   II–7   V7   IΔ

𝄞 𝄴 ²¹CΔ | ²²F7 * | ²³E–7 | ²⁴A7 * | ²⁵D–7 | ²⁶G7 | ²⁷CΔ ‖
              (II–7)

Take The "A" Train

IΔ   V7/V   II–7   V7   IΔ

𝄞 𝄴 CΔ | ℅ | D7 * | ℅ | D–7 | G7 | CΔ ‖

* nondiatonic chord

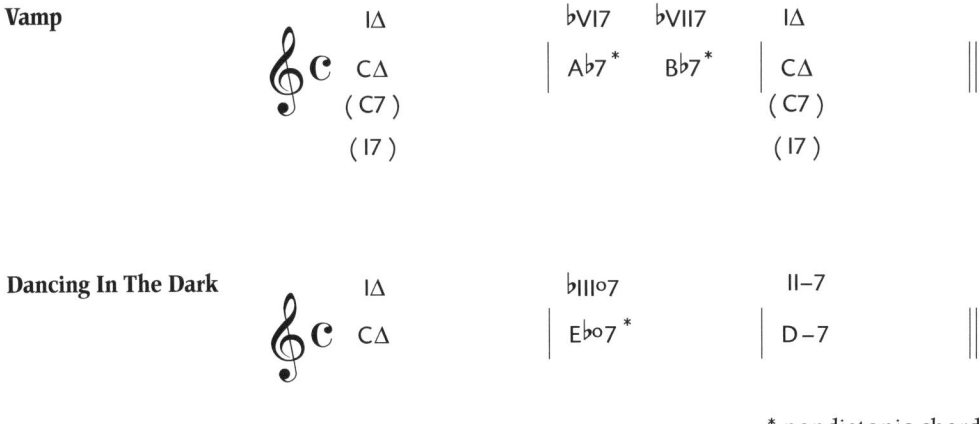

Vamp

	IΔ		♭VI7	♭VII7	IΔ	
	CΔ		A♭7*	B♭7*	CΔ	
	(C7)				(C7)	
	(I7)				(I7)	

Dancing In The Dark

	IΔ		♭III°7		II–7	
	CΔ		E♭°7*		D–7	

* nondiatonic chord

Key-Area Soloing

With certain key-area chord progressions involving limited nondiatonic chord activity, it is possible (and common) to improvise melodies using only the notes of the general key area, *even on the nondiatonic chords.* (For example, you can improvise on the key-area chord progressions shown throughout example 186 using only the C major scale to derive the melody notes.) This is called *key-area soloing* and is especially common in improvised solos on blues progressions, "I Got Rhythm" progressions, and much of the harmony in standard songs.

Since key-area soloing means improvising using only one scale or key (i.e., modal-style), it can be seen to have two useful purposes:

● to make it easier for beginner and intermediate level improvisers to achieve a basic level of melodic accuracy and mobility when soloing in tempo over diatonic *and* nondiatonic chords, and

● to provide advanced improvisers with a modal approach to soloing as an option to a more precise melodic approach.

However, not knowing how to solo inside the nondiatonic chords of a progression in tempo is probably the most fundamental musical obstacle in the improviser's path. Advancing in certain areas will be difficult (and maybe even impossible) as long as this problem exists.

Soloing Inside the Outside Chords

The basic rule for improvising inside a nondiatonic chord is as follows:

To identify a nondiatonic chord in a key-area progression with an improvised melody line alone (i.e., without relying on harmonic accompaniment), the soloist must play at least one of the chord tones which makes the chord nondiatonic to the key-area of the moment.

For example, the chord tones of the A dominant 7th chord (A7) are: A (root), C♯ (major 3rd), E (perfect 5th), and G (minor 7th). Therefore, when the A7 chord occurs in a chord progression in the key-area of C major, the soloist must play the note C♯ at some point during the A7's duration since C♯ is the only chord tone of A7 which is nondiatonic to the key of C major (i.e., A, E and G are diatonic to the key of C major and, in this context, will not clearly and unmistakably identify the A7 chord without relying on harmonic accompaniment.)

Example 187

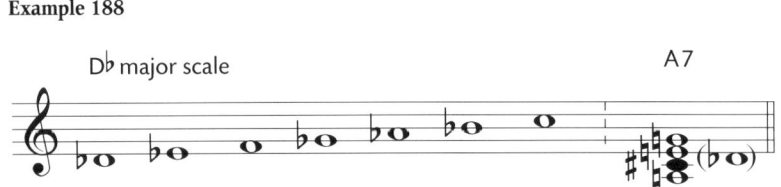

The melody line may, of course, include other notes from the A7 chord or chord scale as well, but the chord tone C♯ is essential to establish the distinct sound of A7 *in the key of C major* using the soloist's melody line alone. The C♯ may be featured in the melody as a prominent note or as a passing tone, as long as it is noticeable by ear.

The important chord tone to play, therefore, on an A7 chord in the key of C major is C♯. However, if the A7 chord were to happen in the key of D♭ major, the important chord tones to play on the A7 chord would be A, E and/or G, because these notes are nondiatonic to the key of D♭ major, whereas C♯ is enharmonically the same note as D♭, and, therefore, is diatonic.

Example 188

Other examples are as follows:

- On an F–7 chord (F, A♭, C, E♭) in the key of C major, the soloist must play the chord tones A♭ and/or E♭, along with any other desirable notes.

- On an E7 chord (E, G♯, B, D) in the key of C major, the soloist must play the chord tone G♯.

- On a Dmaj7 chord in the key of E major, the important chord tone to play is D.

- On a B⌀ chord in the key of F major, the important chord tone is B.

- On a D♭7 chord in the key of E♭ major, the important chord tones are D♭ and C♭.

When the chord tones which are nondiatonic to the key of the moment are *not* played in the melody on their corresponding chords (which is often the case in key-area soloing), the melody line – played by itself – tends to sound ambiguous or non-descriptive of the harmony, and, because of this, suggests that the soloist might be incompetent in this area. (That is, unless it is being done on purpose by an advanced player.) Therefore, intentionally eliminating colorful nondiatonic notes in improvised melody lines as a special effect (i.e., modal-style soloing) is only effective when done *after* one has first demonstrated the ability to solo inside the nondiatonic chords well.

Soloists who have the ability to establish the song's harmony completely and effortlessly through their improvised melodies are no longer dependent on the accompanying players for help in this regard. Consequently, they are free to explore other important aspects of improvisation related to execution, content and shaping the solo more musically.

Exercises

1. (CD 2)

   Write out the chord progression of a standard song, e.g., "Ladybird." Analyze the chord progression using Roman numerals and identify all nondiatonic chords (including those involved in modulations to other keys) by circling their chord symbols.

   Note: When practicing at a medium or fast tempo (e.g., quarter note = 120 or faster), beginner and intermediate level players may eliminate all the II–7 chords contained in II–7 V7 progressions from the song's harmony *when the duration of the II–7 chord is less than four beats*. Replace each eliminated II–7 chord with the related (or following) V7 chord in order to reduce the harmonic detail of the chord progression and lessen the challenge to the soloist.

Example 189

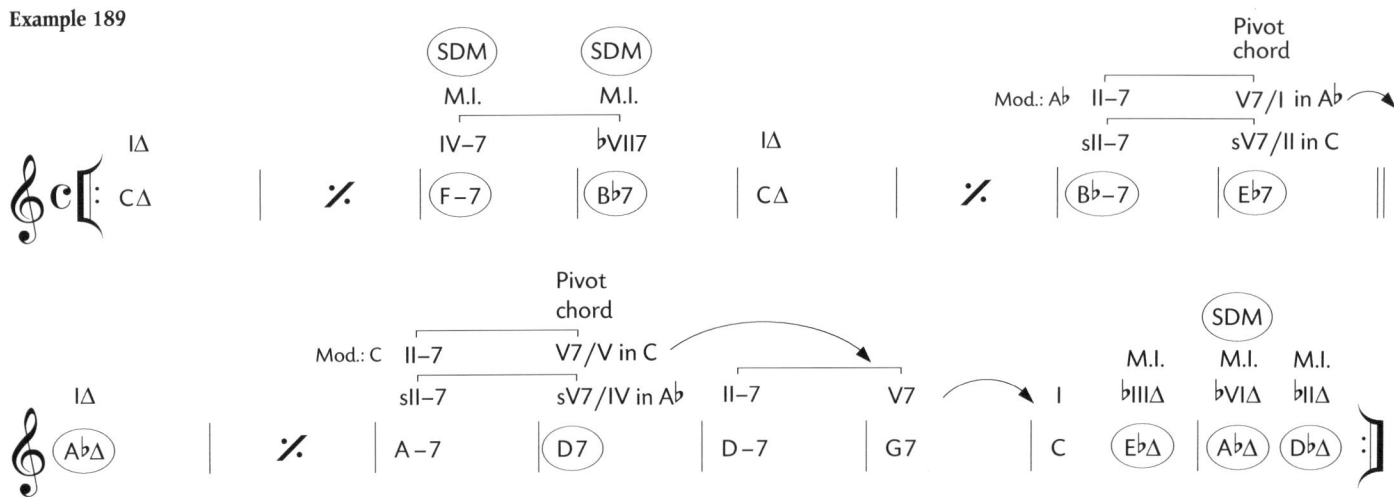

Next, in the staff and underneath the written chord progression, write only those chord tones (of each nondiatonic chord in the progression) which are nondiatonic to the key-area of the moment. Practice soloing on the chords (with and without accompaniment) while including one or more of these nondiatonic notes in the improvised melody line on the corresponding chords.

Note: To better target these notes in your solos, restrict the rhythm to quarter notes only at first, or select a rhythm motive (see page 28), then advance to 8th notes only, and finally to any rhythms.

Example 190

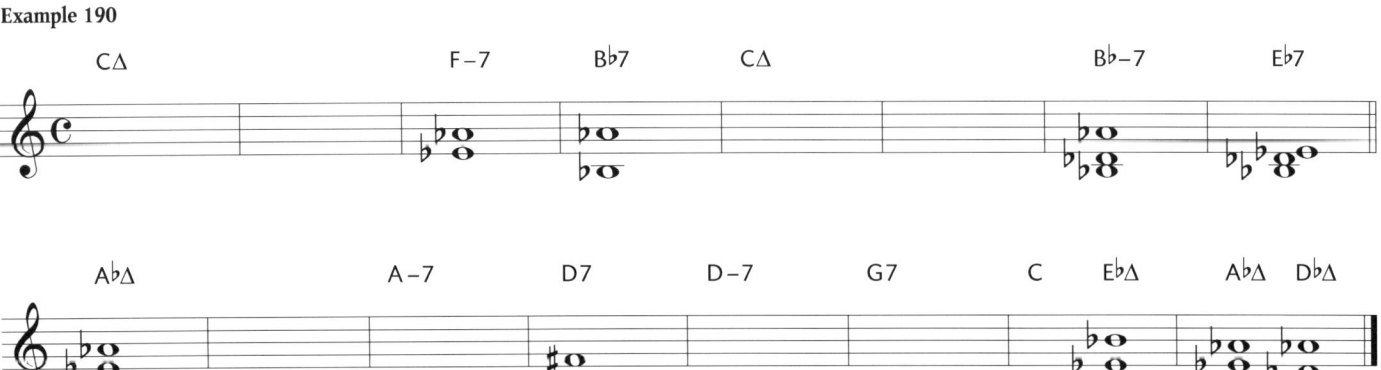

To go a step further, identify those chord tones (of the surrounding *diatonic* chords) which move to and from the nondiatonic notes by step (minor 2nd or major 2nd interval). Write these notes in the stave also to observe and play while soloing. The result will be a guide-tone line, which, when played with the root motion line of the song's harmony, will produce an accurate melodic outline of the song's essential harmony. (See HOW TO IMPROVISE: GUIDE TONES.)

Example 191

(Solo based on above example.)

Players must first be able to clearly outline a song's changing harmony (without depending on harmonic accompaniment) by playing an improvised melody line using the necessary chord tones *before* trying to improvise using chord scales and other challenging techniques. Remember: Preparation is the key to making progress.

• Record and critique your practice daily.

11. Musical Impact

Note: Musical impact is a subject which may only be suitable for practice by players at intermediate and advanced levels of development. However, beginner level players should be able to understand (if not apply) the concept and postpone practicing the exercises until they are more experienced improvisers (see 16. SELF-CRITIQUING – STAGES OF MUSICAL DEVELOPMENT, page 283).

Musical impact happens in an improvised solo when the soloist features a certain element or aspect of the music for a while and then changes to its opposite, or some other contrasting material. This playing strategy invariably attracts the listener's attention and demonstrates the improviser's ability to control the direction of the solo by manipulating musical elements and ideas.

Creating impact in an improvised solo requires two opposing but related actions:

* building tension, and

* releasing it.

Tension can be created and intensified in an improvised solo through repetition; that is, the soloist intentionally repeats and embellishes one (or more) aspect(s) of the content and/or execution of the music until it becomes recognizable as important thematic material.

Tension is released when the player stops repeating/embellishing the selected aspect of the music and introduces its polar opposite, or some other contrasting material. Musical impact happens at the moment when the tension is released, i.e., at the point when the soloist changes from one aspect to its opposite.

An obvious and familiar example can be seen in the area of volume control, or dynamics. The soloist plays softly until this attracts sufficient attention (it may be for one phrase or for an entire chorus or more) and then (s)he suddenly plays loudly. Impact is heard or realized at the moment the music changes from soft to loud.

The change from soft to loud can also occur gradually versus suddenly. Sudden change creates greater surprise which, depending on the musical context, may or may not be desirable. The reverse situation is also possible, i.e., the soloist plays at a consistently loud volume and then suddenly (or gradually) changes to soft playing to create an impact.

Creating and intensifying musical tension, therefore, can be achieved through repetition, which, of course, takes time to happen, and the longer the tension (repetition) is sustained or continued the stronger the impact will be upon its release (change), especially if the release happens timely and suddenly.

It is also possible to overdo the tension and miss the optimal point(s) of resolution. Sometimes this is done on purpose, meaning that the soloist intentionally sustains the tension indefinitely or throughout the entire solo for effect, without actually releasing it in the conventional way. Typically, the strongest musical impact occurs in an improvised solo when tension is created and intensified over a long period of time (such as one chorus or longer), and then released suddenly at a point which coincides with the beginning of a major section of the song's form.

In certain cases it is also important that the build-up and release of tension is supported by the accompanying players, especially with a very noticeable and effective topic such as dynamics. Other more subtle topics, such as phrase lengths, however, require little or no support from the accompanying players, although experienced, imaginative accompanying players will usually find something effective to play in such cases.

The soloist's playing must, therefore, send clear, obvious musical signals to the accompanying players, who, in turn, must be listening closely to the soloist for direction. For this purpose the soloist should exaggerate the execution of whatever musical elements are being used to create the tension and the release, and continue to do so until the accompanying players notice the idea and endeavor to support it.

Musical Topics (with Polar Opposites) Used to Create Impact

Work with each of the topics listed below individually at first, using the exercises below. Then, for optimal results, practice combining individual topics below with topic #1 (dynamics), since changing the volume of the music will always help to create clear, noticeable impact. (See How to Improvise for more information on these topics.)

- Dynamics (soft versus loud)
- Phrase Lengths (short versus long)
- Rhythmic Activity (sparse versus dense)
- Tempo (actual versus double-time or half-time)
- Continuity (motive development versus through-composed)
- Melodic Lyricism (tonal or harmonic versus non-tonal or nonharmonic)
- Pacing (play with no rest versus play a little/rest a lot)
- Register (high versus low)
- Rhythmic Feel (swing versus straight or even)
- Meter (rhythmically defined versus "floating" or rhythmically undefined)
- Articulation (staccato versus legato)

Exercises

- In four steps (CD 1 and/or 2):

  1. Select a topic from the above list. Be sure you have the ability to control each individual part of the polar opposites before trying to use them together to create impact in an improvised solo.

  2. Select a familiar harmonic setting (e.g., a single chord, chord pattern or tune progression), a comfortable tempo, and a preferred mode of accompaniment.

     Note: A play-along recording featuring full rhythm section accompaniment will work fine for these exercises, except that the proper support will not necessarily happen when you build and release tension. This, however, should not deter you from practicing these exercises with play-along recordings.

  3. Improvise a solo while featuring only one aspect of the selected topic for one full chorus (i.e., one full time through the song's form, or approximately one minute), then feature its polar opposite for the next chorus.

     For example, with dynamics as the topic, play very softly for one complete chorus, then change suddenly (or gradually) to loud playing at the beginning of the next chorus and continue playing loudly for one more chorus. (Resting between phrases is okay with a topic such as dynamics provided you play at the proper volume level continuously when you *do* play.) Remember to exaggerate the execution of each aspect in a pair of opposites, e.g., with dynamics, play *very* softly (but with shading), then play *very* loudly (also with shading).

4. Repeat this procedure for eight to ten choruses. Record and critique your solos, focusing criticism only on the objective of the exercise – which is to create a dramatic (or at least a noticeable) musical impact at the beginning of each chorus.

♦ (CD 1 and/or 2)

Repeat exercise above but change step 3 to 1/2 *chorus* (or approximately 1/2 minute) instead of one full chorus, in order to create musical impact at the beginning and mid-point of the song's form every chorus.

♦ (CD 1 and/or 2)

Repeat first exercise but change step 3 to one *section* of the song's form (approximately 15 seconds) instead of one full chorus, in order to create musical impact at the beginning of each section of the song's form every chorus.

♦ (CD 1 and/or 2)

Repeat exercises above but use a new or different topic (i.e., other than dynamics) to create each successive musical impact in the solo.

For example, create the 1st impact (tension/release) of the solo using dynamics (soft/loud); create the 2nd impact of the solo using phrase lengths (short/long); create the 3rd impact of the solo using rhythmic activity (sparse/dense); the 4th impact of the solo using pacing (play/rest); the 5th impact using continuity (motive development/through-composed); the 6th using rhythmic feel (straight/swing); the 7th using articulation (staccato/legato); the 8th using melodic lyricism (non-tonal/tonal); the 9th using meter (rhythmically undefined/defined); the 10th using tempo (actual/double-time); the 11th using register (low/high), etc.

Remember to exaggerate the execution of each aspect of a pair of opposites in order to maximize the musical impact when the tension is released.

♦ Record and critique your practice daily.

Part FOUR: PRACTICING

"Practice is the best of all instructors."

– Publius Syrus
First century B.C.

12. Self-Recording: A Mirror for Your Ears

If you are a beginner or intermediate level improviser, most if not all of your energy and concentration will necessarily be used merely to execute the music of your improvised solos accurately; in other words, to play the right notes at the right time. This means that while you are soloing – whether on the bandstand or in the practice room – you will have very little energy and attention available for observing the results of your playing.

The basic problem with this situation is that if you do not observe the musical results of your improvising closely *while you are playing*, then self-improvement will be very difficult or even impossible because you will not be aware of the specific areas in which you need to improve, or the degree to which you need to improve them. Because if you cannot (or do not) recognize the specific musical problems in your improvising while you are playing, how can you expect to be able to remember specifically what they are afterwords and correct them? This is perhaps the most critical issue regarding making daily progress with your improvising.

Observation produces awareness, without which you cannot learn. Of course, a knowledgeable and observant private jazz teacher can make you aware of specific weaknesses in your improvising during a lesson; but how deep does such awareness go in *you*? And how long does it last for *you*? And how much does this awareness benefit *you* – considering that it only happens periodically, and only through observations made by someone else? This is a precarious way to make progress, and yet it is the usual scenario, unless you bring a private teacher with you into the practice room every day! Or, a tape recorder.

I often find that a good (or even fair) instrumentalist does not need greater technical ability to become a better improviser. Of course, greater technique will certainly help, but right now what the player needs is a deeper or more acute awareness of what his/her improvising sounds like compared to what it *should* sound like. And this comparison can only be made and understood from regularly observing and analyzing both the self-model and a superior one.

Recording and critiquing your practicing daily will give you an opportunity to discover all the important details (both positive and negative) in your improvising, and, as a result, give you an accurate musical self-impression. In this sense, a recording functions like *a mirror for your ears*, one in which you can hear the true "reflection" of your improvising.

Note: Plus, it is much easier to stop playing certain phrases, ideas and effects that you decide you do not particularly like once you have heard yourself play them numerous times on recordings. So, listen to the good results a few times, but listen to the weak results over and over again, because from this you will learn the most, and also retain your humility.

I recommend that you practice a topic of improvising for several minutes and then listen to the recording of your practicing for the next few minutes. In other words, play your instrument for roughly two thirds of your total practice time, and listen/critique your playing for one third. You will surely learn more from this approach (especially if you are a beginner or intermediate-level player) than if you play your instrument for the entire time, in other words, without doing the listening and critiquing. You may discover through listening that you've been practicing a topic or exercise wrongly, or that you've been making hitherto unnoticed mistakes. It is precisely this kind of discovery that makes self-improvement possible.

Many hours of practicing can be wasted simply because you aren't completely clear about the musical results of your improvising. When you play something correctly and you know it is correct, that is successful practicing. And when you play something incorrectly and you know it is incorrect (which can be quite common with improvising), this also is practicing, if less successful. But when you play something correctly or incorrectly and you're not sure whether it is correct or incorrect, this is not practicing at all. As far as your musical development is concerned, this is an unfortunate and unnecessary waste of time.

From only a few minutes of focused, analytical listening to a recording of your improvising, you can realize the *actual* (versus imagined) degree of ability and control you have with a certain topic and exercise in a particular musical context. If you're struggling just to play accurately, you may also be assuming that everything else is okay when it isn't, or that it is all wrong when it isn't! And you may never discover what the truth is if your practicing only involves playing, without listening to the recorded play-backs.

Besides, how much benefit do you actually get from only a few additional minutes of practicing or playing? Not that much, of course, or not enough to make you a better player, especially when you compare that to spending the same amount of time observing and critiquing your recorded solos. With a recording of your solo you can learn to hear for yourself exactly how accurately and musically you did or did not improvise with a topic. Through a recording you can begin to hear your playing as a teacher hears it, i.e., with full attention. Then you will be able to identify some of your specific problems as well, or at least become more familiar with what you play and how you play it. This may even reduce the need you have for a teacher.

Such knowledge then enables you to adjust the background settings of your practicing if necessary (i.e., the tempo, the chord progression, and the accompaniment) so that you can *practice at the edge of your ability* continuously, and thereby obtain greater benefit from each exercise. It also enables you to target certain aspects of your improvising in order to obtain or improve specific skills, and thereby take control over your own improvement without having to depend entirely on a teacher's advise. After all, the reason you need a teacher is only because you cannot – or *do* not – do the job yourself.

With the help of a tape recorder you could quite possibly become one of the best teachers you will ever have, if only because: *Who* cares more about your music than you do? I mean, sure, your music teachers may care a lot, but you cannot expect anyone to care more about you or your music than you do! Except maybe your mother. But let's face it, even if your mother *does* care more about you and your music than you do, what are the chances that underneath that warm, kind-hearted, loving exterior, she is a cold-blooded, self-centered, world-class jazz pedagogue? As far as your list of greatest teachers is concerned, therefore, you should aspire to someday find yourself and your trustworthy tape recorder at the top.

Important

With jazz improvisation, it should come as no surprise that the best listeners – versus the best players – make the best improvisers. In fact, the primary thing that makes advanced improvisers so advanced is that they have the ability to hear themselves in relation to their musical surroundings *while they are improvising*. They perceive the details of this relationship acutely, also, which enables them to continuously adjust and control their playing on a moment by moment basis, similar to driving a car with your eyes open and focused on the road ahead.

But when less evolved players improvise, they barely have enough musical control to hear themselves alone (or the accompaniment alone), never mind the ability to hear themselves in relation to the accompaniment, and therefore they cannot perceive the results of this relationship while they play. Obviously, this makes it very difficult to respond appropriately and effectively to the surroundings, like trying to drive a car with your eyes closed!

So then, until you can clearly hear yourself in relation to the musical surroundings *as* you play, you must do it *after* you play, i.e., through a recording. This is the reason why recording your practice solos and critiquing the playbacks is vitally important. And, even though advanced players may not need to hear/study recordings of their improvising as often as less experienced players do, they will perhaps benefit from the practice even moreso because their highly developed hearing ability will enable them to notice and learn from all aspects of their playing.

If at first you feel anxious or insecure about listening to recordings of your improvising every day, remember that *no one* sounds as good as (s)he ultimately could sound when playing something new and difficult. In fact, those who never struggle or never sound weak in the practice room are either never playing anything new and difficult, or have learned how to *practice at the edge of their ability*. Playing badly, in the case of playing something new, is either an indication that you are a beginner in this particular area, or that you are trying to practice *beyond* your edge of ability. So, don't confuse being an innocent beginner with being an unforgivable wretch of a player!

Continuing to play badly may be an indication that you aren't practicing the right material, or the same material every day in a productive way (i.e., with appropriate harmonic settings, tempos and modes of accompaniment), and not necessarily that you aren't practicing enough, or that you aren't capable of producing positive results. It is important that you can tell the difference.

Suppose you were studying photography. Would you practice taking pictures all day long and then *not* develop the film because you were afraid that the results might be bad? How could you expect to improve or reach your full potential as a photographer without viewing the pictures you take? This is similar to not recording your solos, or to recording your solos but not listening to the playbacks.

With photography it's obvious that you would not learn very much without knowing and understanding the actual (versus imagined) results of your efforts. It's the same when practicing improvisation, especially with beginner and intermediate-level players practicing a specific topic or exercise. Think of a musical topic as a target you are trying to hit or a subject you are exploring with your improvising, and examine the recorded results with the detached, objective attitude of a scientist. True, this requires a certain degree of psychological maturity, but remember – anything that demands strength will also develop strength. And, since listening daily to recordings of your improvising demands and exercises your self-acceptance and self-criticism, it will further develop these capabilities in you as well.

Taking a scientific approach as well as an artistic approach toward learning and practicing music always yields the best results. (See PART III: TARGET PRACTICE, pages 13-52.) You must be a scientist *and* an artist to do music as well as it can be done. Consider how mathematicians who arrive at the wrong answer to a problem are always eager to discover what their mistakes are, because they realize that knowing what their mistakes are will ultimately lead them to the correct answer. They may criticize themselves for making an error, but they feel happy (and relieved also) when they discover it. They are not consumed by feelings of self-doubt when being self-critical. On the contrary, they typically feel inspired and encouraged because they were able to locate, identify and correct their mistakes.

Such is the way to criticize your improvising also: Be glad you have the capability to identify your mistakes. Remember that there was a time when you couldn't! Listen for your mistakes eagerly. Know that in time you will be able to correct them and someday perhaps even avoid them altogether. Be critical of your errors, then, as a mathematician or scientist would, but don't take it personally! Relate to the mistakes you hear on recordings of your improvising as if they were made by someone else.

It is also fair to limit your criticism to only the area or topic targeted by the exercise. For example, when practicing a particular aspect of execution do not be too critical of other aspects of execution, or of the content of the improvising. Understandably, these areas of your solo may sound weaker than usual because you are concentrating on a single aspect of execution only.

It is certainly okay – even helpful – to notice other aspects of your playing which need attention on the recording, but do not let these aspects distract you from observing and critiquing the targeted one. You must keep the immediate objective of your practicing (i.e., the target – the selected topic and exercise) in focus while listening to the recorded playbacks, and avoid being overwhelmed by other discovered strengths or weaknesses.

Typically, your practice solos will sound much less like the finished product when you use the target approach compared to when you do not use it. This is normal and may be expected. Do not insist, therefore, on trying to play the most mind-blowing solo you possibly can when using the target approach. In this context it is wise to just let practice be practice. The time you spend practicing improvisation, therefore, should be divided between (1) using the target method – where you condition yourself to respond accurately and musically within certain restrictions in order to build the musical strengths needed to perform well on the bandstand (similar to the way an athlete exercises to build muscles needed to play a sport well), and (2) improvising normally – or without extra restrictions (similar to the way an athlete plays a sport). Both methods of practicing are necessary.

Sooner or later even your target practice will start to sound like the finished product, so be sure to record and critique both types of practicing mentioned above and compare the results. The answers to most if not all of your musical problems are waiting for you right there on tape.

Exercise

• Obtain two portable audio cassette recorders with internal play-back speakers. These can be purchased for as little as $50.00 each, unless you want them to actually record and play back! Use one to record your practicing and soloing and the other to play the various play-along cassettes (or tapes of play-along CDs) used as the accompaniment for your improvised solos. Purchase several good quality cassette tapes (High Position or High Bias) to use and re-use for recording your practicing.

• Next, locate and arrange your practice area and materials so that you can record your daily practicing as easily and conveniently as possible.

   Note: This step is much more important than it may seem to you right now; try not to overlook it.

• Establish the routine of recording all or some of your practicing every day for observation and critique. (See 13. SELF-CRITIQUING, pages 58-73.) Reserve one cassette tape for recording your improvising with the same topic and exercise once every two weeks or so for the purposes of self-comparison, and also to record your soloing without a specific topic or exercise. This will enable you to measure and document your improvement over time.

   Note: I recommend that you critique the recordings of your practice solos immediately after you record them. However, you can always listen to them at a later time, if necessary, as long as it happens sometime within the next day or so.

13. Self-Critiquing: Accuracy and Musicality

To critique your improvising you must first record yourself soloing in a particular musical context (i.e., in a selected harmonic setting, at a certain tempo, with or without accompaniment), and then judge your playing according to its accuracy and musicality. Remember that the particular musical context you use will have a significant impact on the level of accuracy and musicality you achieve. (See ahead to Musical Contexts for Stages of Development, page 67.)

When critiquing recordings of your improvised solos, the two most fundamental concerns are tempo agreement (time) and chord agreement (chord changes), otherwise known as *time and changes*.

Since an improvised solo can be accurate (i.e., technically correct) in one of these areas without necessarily being musical (i.e., artistically appealing) in that area, but it cannot be musical in this area without first being accurate, accuracy must be considered the primary condition of musicality. (The exception being in the "free" jazz idiom, where the conventional restrictions of tempo and chords do not apply.) Musicality includes accuracy, in other words, but also goes beyond it.

Therefore, the accuracy – or technical correctness – of your improvising in the areas of time and chord changes should be evaluated *separately from and before* any other musical considerations regarding these or other areas.

The musicality – or artistic merit and appeal – of your improvising in any particular area needs to be assessed, therefore, only after accuracy in the basic areas of time and chord changes has been confirmed.

Accuracy (Time, Chord Changes and Exercise Restrictions)

The accuracy of an improvised solo is judged by assessing the *technical correctness* of the improvising within a particular musical context, the main areas of concern being:

● the selection of melody notes played on the chords, and

● the rhythmic placement of these melody notes in time (or tempo).

In other words, time and chord changes. (For drummers, accuracy in the area of chord changes means marking all major subdivisions of the song's compositional form, e.g., AABA, with audible rhythmic punctuations, usually prepared by drum fills.)

Since the right (or correct) melody notes can be played in the wrong (or incorrect) time, and the wrong melody notes can be played in the right time, complete accuracy, per se, means that the right melody notes must be played in the right time. (See next page for further explanation.)

Important

When assessing practice solos that feature a selected topic and exercise (i.e., target practice – featuring topics such as pacing, phrase lengths, rhythmic feel, etc.), accuracy must include assessing the technical correctness of your improvising regarding any and all restrictions or exercise instructions that may be involved *in addition to the time and chord changes*, (e.g., pacing: play two measures, rest two measures; phrase lengths: play short phrases only; rhythmic feel: use swing feel only, etc.). If such restrictions are not observed throughout the solo, the improvising cannot be considered to be completely accurate.

The Right Melody Notes

Playing the right melody notes on the chords means playing notes which are

- harmonic to the chord or chord scale (i.e., chord tones and available tensions), or

- *nonharmonic* to the chord but which resolve directly or indirectly by 1/2 step to harmonic notes, usually within the chord's duration – or, which move in such a way as to sound resolved. (Drummers must mark all major subdivisions of the song's form.)

Ideally, the essential sounds of the harmony (or, for drummers: the compositional form) of the song should be recognizable by ear from the improvised melody line alone, i.e., without depending on harmonic support from the accompaniment.

If the soloist plays on a *nondiatonic* chord, therefore, (s)he must play at least one of the chord tones which make the chord nondiatonic to the key of the moment.

For example, on an A7 chord in the key of C major, the soloist must play a C♯ in the melody since C♯ is the only chord tone of A7 (A, C♯, E, G) which is nondiatonic to the key of C, and, therefore, the only chord tone which will identify the A7 chord in this harmonic setting when there is no accompaniment.

On A7 in the key of D♭, however, the soloist must play an A, an E, and/or a G in the melody, since these are the chord tones of A7 which are nondiatonic to the key of D♭, and which will identify the chord in this harmonic setting when there is no accompaniment.

For the purpose of assessing your improvising, then, at least one such essential note must be played (either as a prominent note or a passing tone) on a nondiatonic chord during at least one of its occurrences or the improvising is not considered to be melodically accurate – especially if the nondiatonic chord is one of only a few in the entire progression. (See 10. INSIDE THE OUTSIDE CHORDS, page 43.)

The Right Time

Playing melody notes in the right time means playing rhythms in which the downbeat and upbeat attacks of the improvised melody coincide more or less exactly with those produced by the accompaniment.

Ideally, both the intended tempo and meter (time signature) of the music should be recognizable by ear from the improvised melody line alone, i.e., without depending on rhythmic support from the accompaniment.

The Restrictions

Playing within the restrictions of a selected topic and exercise means that the restrictions should be clear and obvious throughout the improvised solo, i.e., recognizable by ear from the improvised melody line alone.

Note: To isolate your improvising so that the time, chord changes and exercise restrictions can be assessed without the accompaniment, use one tape recorder to record your playing while you listen to the play-along accompaniment (played on another machine) through ear phones. The recording of your improvising will contain only your solo, i.e., without the accompaniment.

If your improvising is not accurate in one of the above mentioned areas (i.e., time, chord changes, and – when applicable – the exercise restrictions), it should not be further judged for musicality in this area. In this case, continue to practice improvising while focusing on accuracy. Musicality should follow eventually.

Musicality (Content, Execution, Pacing, Technique)

The musicality of an improvised solo is judged by assessing the artistic merit and appeal of your improvising within a particular musical context, the main concern here being your ability to manipulate and control (i.e., *balance*) the various elements of content (what to play), execution (how to play), and pacing (when to play), and to do so with notable instrumental technique. (See the topical list below for examples.)

Topics to Assess for Musicality in Improvised Solos

It is important to remember that the musicality (artistic appeal) of your improvising is judged by assessing how well you control *(balance)* the various aspects of each topic. For explanations and exercises regarding the topics listed below, see 5. EXECUTION, book I, page 85, 6. CONTENT, book I, page 111, and 11. MUSICAL IMPACT, page 50. Also see HOW TO IMPROVISE: PACING, PHRASE LENGTHS, RHYTHMIC DENSITY, MOTIVE DEVELOPMENT and NONHARMONIC MELODY NOTES.

By referencing each of the topics below with a number, specific problems or weaknesses noticed in your improvising can be indicated by number on the Improvisation Assessment Chart. (See IMPROVISATION ASSESSMENT CHART on page 71.) This will enable you to document and track your progress as well as make more informed decisions regarding the topics you are practicing now and those topics you should practice next.

Content (What to Play)

Melody

1. **Melodic functions** (balancing the use of chord tones, harmonic tensions and nonharmonic notes properly resolved in the melody).

2. **Melodic lyricism** (balancing the use of singable and non-singable pitch sequences in the melody).

3. **Melodic curve** (balancing the use of stepwise motion, repeated notes and leaps in the melody line, in both upward and downward directions).

4. **Melodic phrase lengths** (balancing the use of short, medium and long phrases).

5. **Melodic style** (balancing the use of vocabulary licks and melodic patterns with creative and imaginative ideas).

6. **Melodic continuity** (balancing the use of motive development with through-composed melody).

   Note: Motive development means repeating or embellishing thematic elements of previously played melodic ideas. Through-composed melody means avoiding any recognizable repetition or embellishment of thematic elements from previously played phrases.(See HOW TO IMPROVISE, MOTIVE DEVELOPMENT.)

Rhythm

7. **Rhythmic forward motion** (balancing the use of syncopated rhythms – i.e., upbeat attacks either followed by a rest on the next downbeat or sustained over the beat line – with non-syncopated rhythms).

8. **Rhythmic activity** (balancing the use of sparse rhythmic activity – i.e., notes of long duration, e.g., dotted quarters, half notes, whole notes, etc. – with dense rhythmic activity – i.e., notes of short duration, e.g., 8ths, triplets, sixteenths, etc.).

Execution (How to Play)

9. **Rhythmic feel** (balancing the use of swing feel, even feel and double-time feel).

10. **Accents** (balancing the use of downbeat accents and ghost notes with upbeat accents and ghost notes).

11. **Articulation** (balancing the use of legato articulation with staccato).

12. **Dynamics – natural and general** (balancing the use of soft, medium and loud volume levels within each measure, phrase and section of music).

13. **Special effects** (balancing moderate with extreme use of musical effects, e.g., vibrato).

Pacing (When to Play)

14. **Resting between melodic phrases** (balancing the use of space or non-activity between melodic phrases, with regard for duration and frequency).

Instrumental Technique

15. **Sound quality.**

16. **Intonation.**

17. **Flexibility.**

18. **Register control.**

19. **Range.**

20. **Endurance.**

21. **Unique aspects of a certain type of instrument.**

Other Areas to Consider

22. **Interacting with the accompaniment** (e.g., leading, following, adjusting, etc.).

23. **Recovering from mistakes** (e.g., getting lost in the song's form while soloing).

24. **Improvising by ear** (i.e., without reading the chords or knowing what they are).

When assessing your improvising, keep in mind that judging accuracy means assessing the technical correctness of the improvising regarding

- the selection of melody notes,
- the rhythmic placement of the melody notes in time, and
- the exercise restrictions (if any).

Judging musicality means assessing the particular *balance* achieved in the solo regarding the various aspects of content, execution and pacing, as well as the quality of instrumental technique demonstrated in the solo.

And remember: Specific problems or weaknesses in the content, execution, pacing and instrumental technique of your improvising can be indicated on the IMPROVISATION ASSESSMENT CHART under TOPIC NUMBERS using the corresponding topic number from the above list.

More About Accuracy and Musicality

After playing an improvised solo we generally do not prefer to hear a comment such as, "Hey, your playing sounded incredibly accurate on that last tune," or, "Hey, your solo sounded really correct." This is because it is like being told that your playing is incredibly *average*. Of course, we'd really prefer to hear something more like, "Wow, your solo on that last tune blew a hole in my brain!" Meaning that, apparently, somebody with a hole in his/her brain thinks your solo was extraordinarily musical and appealing. So, you see, either way – you lose!

To discover the truth about the accuracy and musicality of your playing, therefore, you simply cannot rely on what people in general have to say about it. You must study it for yourself and come to know it extremely well, meaning that you must critique the accuracy and musicality of your improvising on a regular basis, either by yourself or with the help of a teacher or more advanced player.

As I mentioned previously, the ability to play accurately in a certain musical context must happen *before* the ability to play musically can or will happen. In other words, you must be able to play the right notes in the right time on the chords of a song before you can shape these notes into a lyrical, appealing melody line on the chords and execute it expressively. Only when your ability to play accurately in a certain musical context is automatic will you be free to devote energy and attention to playing musically in that context. This rule applies whether you are observing the restrictions of a topic and exercise while you improvise, or not.

Being capable of playing accurately concerning time and changes, therefore, prepares you to transform the level of your improvising from craft (the right notes in the right time) to art (the only notes in the only time!), but it does not guarantee this transformation. Effortless accuracy demonstrated with notable instrumental technique must happen first, and then imagination, creativity, knowledge of tradition, a sense for musical balance, and a certain degree of fearlessness is necessary to shape the various aspects of improvisation into an artistic musical performance.

But how do you increase your accuracy and control over specific areas or topics of improvisation in order to begin working on musicality? The answer lies in applying restrictions to your practicing, by which I mean *to create and practice exercises which restrict your attention to one individual area or topic of improvisation alone throughout a solo.*

Note: This concept of practicing is explored in greater detail in sections 8, 9, 10 and 11.

For example, to develop greater ability with rhythm and rhythmic feel, restrict the melody of the solo to a single pitch while soloing in tempo over a song's chord progression (the root or 5th of the song's key usually works okay, especially on standard songs), and practice controlling the placement of the upbeat, or exaggerating the syncopation, or dynamics, articulations and accents throughout the solo. Or, to develop greater ability with melodic accuracy and lyricism, restrict the rhythm of the solo to quarter notes or half notes, etc.

Important

One of the major difficulties encountered when practicing individual topics of improvisation (i.e., target practice), is the overwhelming urge or compulsion we feel to make each improvised solo sound as musical as possible – whether or not we can *first* make it accurate. In other words, due to the underlying misconception that musicality can be achieved before (or without) accuracy, we are unable to divert our attention and efforts away from striving for musicality long enough to achieve sufficient accuracy with the time, chord changes and the exercise restrictions, and, therefore, we fail to make decent progress with the topic. We want the finished product (musicality) without having to pay the necessary price (accuracy).

However, when you consider that the improvised solos of most beginner and intermediate-level players rarely sound like a mature finished product anyway, whether or not they are using the target approach, it becomes clear that these players have no choice other than to work predominantly on accuracy. And, although advanced improvisers are usually capable of improvising accurately and musically in difficult musical contexts, their capability often diminishes dramatically (demonstrating their *true* level of control) when they must also focus on a topic and observe the restrictions of a particular exercise while they improvise.

During your daily improvisation practice, therefore, I recommend that you practice playing solos in which the time, chord changes and restrictions of a topic and exercise are adhered to closely (i.e., solos that are accurate) – *even though your improvising may sound less musical or less like the finished product* – instead of playing solos in which the time, chord changes and exercise restrictions are eventually forgotten or ignored altogether. Then, to create a balanced daily practice routine, you should also spend some time improvising without the additional restrictions of a specific topic and exercise. But remember: Your ability to improvise musically in a particular musical context and with a particular topic comes directly (and only) *after* you have the ability to improvise accurately.

Critiquing Your Improvising

When critiquing recordings of your improvised solos, listen *first* to discover the level of accuracy you have achieved regarding playing within the restrictions of the selected topic and exercise. Recognizing such accuracy (or inaccuracy) in your playing may require the help of a teacher or a more advanced improviser at first, because beginner and intermediate level players often have a limited capacity to hear and recognize specific details in their playing, even when listening to recordings of their solos. (We hear only that which we *can* hear. See 3. EAR TRAINING, book I, page 73.) In order to notice these details more acutely, therefore, you must continually ask yourself what it is that you do not already hear in the music while you listen to it.

This situation can be improved by knowing specifically what to listen for and then practice listening for and to these details every day. And, while listening, always assume that it is possible to hear more details in the music, and to hear them more acutely than you currently can, and sooner or later you will! An important key to improving your hearing ability, in other words, is to reject the idea that your hearing is already good enough as it is, and to accept the idea that it can always be improved. Remember: The best *listeners* make the best improvisers.

If you hear on a self-recording that your accuracy with a particular topic and exercise during a practice solo is good and was easily achieved in all or most respects, listen again to the recording to discern the level of accuracy achieved regarding the time and chord changes. If the level of accuracy here is also high and was easily achieved, listen several more times to discern the level of musicality achieved regarding the various aspects of content, execution, pacing and instrumental technique.

However, if the level of accuracy is low concerning the selected topic, or the time, or the changes, or if the accuracy required maximum effort to achieve, do not bother to critique the musicality of the solo and continue to practice accuracy.

For each topic and exercise you choose to practice, remember to select tempos, harmonic settings and modes of accompaniment that are right for you, i.e., settings that enable you to practice at the edge of your ability. If the topic and exercise are challenging, make the settings easy; if the topic and exercise are easy, make the settings challenging; and then let the exercise do its job. (See 14: KNOW THYSELF – HOW AND WHAT TO PRACTICE. Also see the end of this section for exercises on critiquing accuracy and musicality.)

Once you have assessed the accuracy and musicality of your improvising in various musical contexts, it will then be possible to determine your Stage of Musical Development.

Stages of Musical Development (Instrumental and Improvisational)

Since it is not uncommon to find yourself practicing material that may either be too easy or too difficult for your level of ability, determining a reasonably close approximation of your level of ability first (and regularly) will enable you to select topics and design exercises to practice which are appropriate for your level of development, and thereby avoid wasting time in the practice room. As I mentioned earlier, this is a critical aspect of making improvement on a regular basis.

Levels and Sublevels

As you continue to improve as an instrumentalist and improviser, you will gradually pass through the four main Stages of Musical Development:

• Beginner,

• Intermediate,

• Advanced, and

• Master.

One can observe that these four stages of musical development are comparable to the four basic stages in human physical development:

• Infant,

• Child,

• Adolescent, and

• Adult.

The correlation between the four stages of musical development and the four stages of physical growth is significant here as a reminder that you cannot expect an adolescent, or a child, or an infant to behave and perform like an adult. Understanding the parallels between the development of the physical body and that of the musical body will give you a clearer and more realistic idea about where you fit into the larger musical picture, and also about the topics and exercises you should be practicing at your current stage of development (e.g., beginners should be practicing the basics, etc.).

When doing a self-assessment, therefore, keep in mind that even though you may be an adult (or physically mature) human being, you may not be an adult (or musically mature) improviser or instrumentalist. In fact, if you've been practicing jazz improvisation seriously for less than 20 years, you will most likely not be an adult or master level improviser but either an advanced-level improviser, or an intermediate level improviser or a beginner.

Each one of the four main Stages of Musical Development can be further divided into three sublevels of ability:

♦ Beginning,

♦ Intermediate, and

♦ Advanced

producing a total of twelve Stages of Musical Development in all, as demonstrated in the upcoming outline. These logical divisions and subdivisions are helpful to more accurately pinpoint your level of musical ability, not only in major areas of study but with individual topics as well.

For example, in the major practice area of improvisation, or with an individual topic of improvisation such as rhythmic feel, a beginner-level player may be either a *Beginning Beginner* (level 1), an *Intermediate Beginner* (level 2), or an *Advanced Beginner* (level 3), etc.

As you assess your strengths and weaknesses, it may be helpful to consider the following points:

♦ Everyone starts at the beginning and must go through the same stages of development to reach musical maturity and mastery.

♦ The amount of time, practice and experience required to progress from one level to the next regarding specific musical topics is likely to be different for everyone.

♦ You may be advanced in some areas while a beginner in others.

♦ You may be a beginner in all areas while advanced in none.

♦ Regardless of your overall Stage of Musical Development, you will always be at a *beginning* sublevel of ability when learning something new, such as playing in a higher or lower register, soloing at a faster or slower tempo, etc.

♦ Once completed, the entire developmental process can begin again, as in a never-ending cycle or continuum, where old or familiar material is relearned in new ways and at deeper levels.

Important

Assess your level of instrumental and/or improvisational ability with a *specific topic and exercise* once a week according to the upcoming outline. Assess your *general or overall* level of instrumental and/or improvisational ability once a month. (See ASSESSING YOUR IMPROVISING, page 70, and the IMPROVISATION ASSESSMENT CHART, page 71.) Also, don't hesitate to ask a teacher or more advanced player for help with these assessments.

If the Stage of Musical Development you are at is between Beginning Beginner and Advanced Intermediate, you should be concerned primarily with the accuracy of your improvising – especially when practicing specific topics and exercises – and secondarily with musicality. Then, as you progress closer toward the Advanced Stage and beyond with such topics and exercises, increasingly shift your focus toward musicality, creativity and originality.

Stages of Musical Development (The Outline)

The estimated time frames given to each Stage of Musical Development in the outline below are based on my own experience working with serious, career-minded, jazz improvisation students. However, these time frames should be regarded only as a general guide since exceptions can occur at all levels (meaning that playing jazz for 6 years or less doesn't necessarily limit you to being a beginner-level improviser, and also that playing jazz for 20 years or more doesn't automatically make you a master).

- **Beginner** (Accuracy, Some Musicality)

  Infant Stage: 0 to approx. 6 years experience.

  Beginning (Beginning Beginner – BB) 0 to 2 years

  Intermediate (Intermediate Beginner – IB) 2 to 4 years

  Advanced (Advanced Beginner – AB) 4 to 6 years

- **Intermediate** (Accuracy, Musicality)

  Child Stage: Approx. 6 to 12 years experience.

  Beginning (BI) 6 to 8 years

  Intermediate (II) 8 to 10 years

  Advanced (AI) 10 to 12 years

- **Advanced** (Musicality, Creativity)

  Adolescent Stage: 12 to 18 years experience.

  Beginning (BA) 12 to 14 years

  Intermediate (IA) 14 to 16 years

  Advanced (AA) 16 to 18 years

- **Master** (Musicality, Creativity, Originality)

  Adult Stage: 18 (+) years experience.

  Beginning (BM) 18 to 25 years

  Intermediate (IM) 25 to 30 years

  Advanced (AM) 30 or more years

(See end of this section for exercises.)

Musical Contexts for Stages of Development 1-9

Following are suggested musical contexts which correspond to each one of the first nine Stages of Musical Development (Beginning Beginner through Advanced Advanced). Use these musical settings *or your own modified versions* when testing your ability to improvise at a particular level.

In the chart below, both the tempo and the harmonic setting of the musical context increase in difficulty with *each* increase in level (i.e., from level 1 to level 2, from 2 to 3, from 3 to 4, etc.), while the mode of accompaniment increases in difficulty at *every other* increase in level (i.e., from level 2 to 3, from 4 to 5, from 6 to 7, and from 8 to 9).

The tempos listed below for each level do not indicate a range of speeds within which the song could be played for testing purposes, but, rather, the actual slow speed and fast speed at which the song should be played for testing purposes.

Also, the chord progressions of the example tunes listed below may be played with swing or even feel (for testing purposes), and may be transposed to keys other than the original ones in order to increase or decrease the degree of musical challenge. (For additional tune titles see Tune Examples listed in "Harmonic Content of Tunes," next page; also see A. TUNE FILE, extra help, page 2.)

A general description of the harmonic content of the tunes used for each level immediately follows the chart. (For information explaining the harmonic content indicated for each level, see 2. HARMONY, book I, page 31.)

Summary of Musical Contexts for Stages of Development

Use these musical settings *or your own modified versions* when testing your ability to improvise at a particular level.

Level	Tempo	Modes of Accompaniment	Tunes (Harmonic Settings)
1. (BB)	84 (slow)	Full Rhythm Section	So What, Maiden Voyage,
	92 (fast)		Sunflower, Blues in C, F, B♭, G
2. (IB)	80	Full Rhythm Section	All Of Me, Take The A Train,
	100		Satin Doll, Beautiful Love, etc.
3. (AB)	76	Full Rhythm Section	Autumn Leaves, Softly,
	112	Partial Rhythm Section	Easy To Love, Blue Bossa, etc.
4. (BI)	72	Full Rhythm Section	Night And Day, Just Friends,
	126	Partial Rhythm Section	I Love You, Lady Bird, etc.
5. (II)	66	Partial Rhythm Section	Four, Solar, All The Things You Are
	152	Metronome	Alone Together, etc.
6. (AI)	60	Partial Rhythm Section	Joy Spring, Nica's Dream,
	174	Metronome	Stable Mates, Invitation, etc.
7. (BA)	54	Partial Rhythm Section	Inner Urge, Windows,
	200	Metronome, Unaccompanied	Tones For Joan's Bones, etc.
8. (IA)	48	Partial Rhythm Section	Yes Or No, Lazy Bird, ESP,
	220	Metronome, Unaccompanied	Airegin, Cherokee, Lover, etc.
9. (AA)	44	Drums, Metronome	Giant Steps, Count Down,
	240+	Unaccompanied	Moments Notice, 26-2, etc.

Harmonic Content of Tunes Used for Musical Contexts

Level 1: Beginning Beginner

Harmonic setting: Diatonic harmony and/or modal progressions comprised of up to two or three common key areas lasting four or more measures each; simple 12-measure, three-chord blues progressions in C, F, B♭ and G; harmonic material features easy or familiar keys.

Tune examples: **So What, Little Sunflower, Maiden Voyage, C-Jam Blues, Straight No Chaser**. (Also see PLAY-ALONG CD 1).

Level 2: Intermediate Beginner

Harmonic setting: Mostly diatonic harmony; two or three nondiatonic chords (e.g., secondary dominants: V7 of II–7, etc.) lasting four or more beats each; basic 12-measure blues progressions using ♯IV°7 in 6th measure, V7 of II–7 in 8th measure, II–7 in 9th measure, V7 in 10th measure, I7 in 11th measure; easy or familiar keys.

Tune examples: **Beautiful Love, Satin Doll, Take The A Train, Blue Room, Don't Get Around Much Anymore, All Of Me, Now's The Time, Blue Monk.**

Level 3: Advanced Beginner

Harmonic setting: Mostly diatonic harmony; nondiatonic chords (secondary dominants), some at two beats duration; simple modal interchange (IV– to I major or III–, etc.); modulations from common major keys to related *diatonic* minor keys (i.e., from I major to the key of II–, or III–, or VI–, and the reverse); basic 12-measure blues progressions in E♭ and A♭; basic I Got Rhythm progression in C, F and B♭.

Tune examples: **Autumn Leaves, Easy To Love, Blue Bossa, I Hear A Rhapsody, Softly As In A Morning Sunrise, You And The Night And The Music, Nardis, Scrapple From The Apple, Afro Blue, Bessie's Blues, Freddie The Freeloader, Oleo, Anthropology, Cottontail.** (Use keys specified above for blues tunes and I Got Rhythm progressions.)

Level 4: Beginning Intermediate

Harmonic setting: More difficult nondiatonic chords (e.g., substitute dominants: sub V7 of I, II, etc.); secondary dominants; all modal interchange progressions; chromatically altered diatonic chords; modulations from relatively easy major keys to other easy major and minor keys (keys last for two or more measures each); 12-measure blues progressions using sub V7 of V7 in 8th measure and other basic chord substitutions; basic I Got Rhythm progression in more difficult keys (e.g., A♭).

Tune examples: **What Is This Thing Called Love, Night And Day, Just Friends, Lady Bird, Green Dolphin Street, I love You, Out Of Nowhere, There Is No Greater Love, In A Mellow Tone, Yesterdays, Au Privave, Blue Trane, Blues For Alice, All Blues, Equinox.** (Use keys specified above for blues tunes and I Got Rhythm progressions.)

Level 5: Intermediate Intermediate

Harmonic setting: Secondary dominants; substitute dominants; modal interchange; chromatically altered diatonic chords; modulations involving more difficult keys; keys may last for less than two measures each; progressions may contain several modulations; blues and I Got Rhythm progressions in more difficult keys with chord substitutions (e.g., D, A, D♭, B♭ minor, E♭ minor).

Tune examples: **All The Things You Are, Tune Up, There Will Never Be Another You, Four, I'll Remember April, Groovin' High, Like Someone In Love, Alone Together, Well You Needn't, In Your Own Sweet Way, Speak Low, A Night In Tunisia, Someday My Prince Will Come, Solar, Blues, I Got Rhythm,** walking ballads (use keys specified above for blues and I Got Rhythm progressions).

Level 6: Advanced Intermediate

Harmonic Setting: Secondary dominants; substitute dominants; modal interchange; chromatically altered diatonic chords; modulations involving more difficult keys; keys may last for less than two measures each; progressions may contain several modulations; blues progressions in difficult keys with advanced chord substitutions; I Got Rhythm progressions in difficult keys with sub V7 chord substitutions on the bridge.

Tune examples: **Daahoud, Invitation, Nica's Dream, Have You Met Miss Jones, Joy Spring, Stable Mates, Along Came Betty, Conception, Stella By Starlight, Confirmation, Con Alma, UMMG, Up Jumped Spring, Speak No Evil, Bluesette,** walking ballads **(But Beautiful, Body And Soul, I Can't Get Started, Here's That Rainy Day, Angel Eyes)**.

Level 7: Beginning Advanced

Harmonic setting: See level 6 above – ADVANCED INTERMEDIATE, add constant structure (symmetric) harmony.

Tune examples: **Inner Urge, Windows, Tones For Joan's Bones,** slow ballads **(Ruby My Dear, Reflections, Panonica)**.

Level 8: Intermediate Advanced

Harmonic setting: See level 7 above – BEGINNING ADVANCED, add longer song forms (e.g., 64 measure tunes).

Tune examples: **Cherokee, Seven Steps To Heaven, Yes Or No, Lazy Bird, Woody'n You, The Song Is You, Airegin, Lover, Just One Of Those Things, Without A Song, When Your Lover Has Gone, The Way You Look Tonight,** slow ballads **(Central Park West, Infant Eyes, 502 Blues, Waltz)**.

Level 9: Advanced Advanced

Harmonic setting: See level 8 above – INTERMEDIATE ADVANCED, add tonic systems.

Tune examples: **Giant Steps, Moments Notice, Count Down, 26-2,** slow ballads **(Very Early, Iris, Virgo, Pee Wee)**.

(See end of this section for exercises.)

Assessing Your Improvising

The Improvisation Assessment Chart on the following page can be photo-copied multiple times and used in conjunction with the information contained in ACCURACY AND MUSICALITY (page 58), TOPICS TO ASSESS FOR MUSICALITY (page 60), STAGES OF MUSICAL DEVELOPMENT (page 64), and MUSICAL CONTEXTS FOR STAGES OF DEVELOPMENT (page 67) by you and/or your teacher to document and assess your level of improvising, either in general or with selected topics and exercises. (See first exercise at end of this section.)

The following marking system can be used with the assessment chart to rate your improvising:

♦ S = Satisfactory performance.

♦ U = Unsatisfactory performance.

To be successful at any particular level your improvising should be assessed as satisfactory (S) in each of the three categories of Accuracy [(i.e., time, chord changes (song form for drummers) and the topic/exercise], and also in each of the four categories of Musicality (i.e., content, execution, pacing and technique). In other words, if your improvising is assessed as unsuccessful (U) in any one category of accuracy or musicality, your ability has not yet reached the level of that particular musical context.

Improvisation Assessment Chart
(to photocopy)

Date	Topic/Exercise		Current Rating

Song Title (Harmonic Setting)	Level (circle one) 1 2 3 4 5 6 7 8 9	Tempo ♩ = ♩ =	Accompaniment

First Chorus Solo / Second Chorus Solo

Accuracy	Grade	Musicality	Grade	Topic #s	Accuracy	Grade	Musicality	Grade	Topic #s
Time		Content			Time		Content		
Changes		Execution			Changes		Execution		
Form		Pacing			Form		Pacing		
Topic/Ex		Technique			Topic/Ex		Technique		

Third Chorus Solo / Fourth Chorus Solo

Accuracy	Grade	Musicality	Grade	Topic #s	Accuracy	Grade	Musicality	Grade	Topic #s
Time		Content			Time		Content		
Changes		Execution			Changes		Execution		
Form		Pacing			Form		Pacing		
Topic/Ex		Technique			Topic/Ex		Technique		

Date	Topic/Exercise		Current Rating

Song Title (Harmonic Setting)	Level (circle one) 1 2 3 4 5 6 7 8 9	Tempo ♩ = ♩ =	Accompaniment

First Chorus Solo / Second Chorus Solo

Accuracy	Grade	Musicality	Grade	Topic #s	Accuracy	Grade	Musicality	Grade	Topic #s
Time		Content			Time		Content		
Changes		Execution			Changes		Execution		
Form		Pacing			Form		Pacing		
Topic/Ex		Technique			Topic/Ex		Technique		

Third Chorus Solo / Fourth Chorus Solo

Accuracy	Grade	Musicality	Grade	Topic #s	Accuracy	Grade	Musicality	Grade	Topic #s
Time		Content			Time		Content		
Changes		Execution			Changes		Execution		
Form		Pacing			Form		Pacing		
Topic/Ex		Technique			Topic/Ex		Technique		

Exercise 1

Select a topic of improvisation and a particular exercise with appropriate restrictions to use for assessing your improvising. For example, the topic could be dynamics, and the exercise could be to exaggerate the natural dynamics of the melody line (i.e., the accented notes and ghost notes) at the general volume level of soft throughout the solo.

Decide on a particular level from the STAGES OF MUSICAL DEVELOPMENT (page 66) at which to test your ability (e.g., level 3, ADVANCED BEGINNER). Then, from the MUSICAL CONTEXTS FOR STAGES OF DEVELOPMENT (page 67), select a song (i.e., a harmonic setting), a tempo and a mode of accompaniment appropriate for this level of development (e.g., level 3, ADVANCED BEGINNER, "Autumn Leaves," ♩ = 112, bass and drums only or bass line only for accompaniment).

Note: You can make your own partial rhythm section play-along tapes by playing the root motion line of the selected chord progression in half notes on a keyboard (or on your instrument) while setting a metronome to quarter notes.

Write all relevant information on a photocopy of the IMPROVISATION ASSESSMENT CHART (see previous page). When doing a self-assessment without using a specific topic, write the word *general* under or next to the words *Topic/Exercise* on the assessment chart. Under the word *Level*, circle the number that corresponds to the STAGE OF MUSICAL DEVELOPMENT at which you are testing yourself (e.g., for ADVANCED BEGINNER circle the number 3.)

Note: In order to clearly hear and recognize the strengths and weaknesses in your accuracy and musicality with regard to practicing a specific topic, it may be helpful while you are listening to the recording of your improvising to continuously ask yourself one of the following questions:

- Why (specifically) does or doesn't the solo sound accurate and musical?

- How could the solo have been more accurate and musical regarding the (selected) topic and exercise?

- What would have made the (selected) topic and exercise sound more appealing?

- What don't I hear (or what musical details am I not aware of) in the improvising?

Remembering to ask yourself questions such as these throughout your listening will help keep your mind focussed on the selected topic during the critique. You will then notice the relevant musical details of your soloing more accutely as well. This will also become easier to do with practice.

With the recorded accompaniment being played through ear phones (i.e., so only you can hear it), use another machine to record your improvising in the musical context you have selected (with or without reading the music) for one or more times through the song's form. Using the marking system explained above and the Improvisation Assessment Chart, critique *each* chorus of your improvised solo separately, as follows:

- Listen to the recorded playback of your improvising only (i.e., without the accompaniment) to observe and critique your accuracy with the selected topic and exercise (i.e., the restrictions). Indicate the results on the assessment chart.

- Listen again to observe and critique the accuracy of the time and chord changes. (See the beginning of this section on SELF-CRITIQUING for information about judging the accuracy of the time and chord changes.) Indicate the results on the assessment chart.

- Listen again to observe and critique the musicality of the pacing. Indicate the results on the assessment chart. (See TOPICS TO ASSESS FOR MUSICALITY, page 60.)

  Note: A good general rule to follow when assessing the *pacing* in an improvised solo is this: The frequency and duration of your resting (i.e., between phrases) should make the listener want to hear you play, whereas the frequency and duration of your playing should not make the listener want to hear you rest! To prevent the music from sounding too busy, therefore, rest must occur at appropriate intervals (i.e., once or twice every few measures or so, depending on the musical content of the previous phrases and the tempo), and continue for appropriate durations (i.e., from a few beats to a few measures, again depending on the content of the previous phrases and the tempo).

- Listen again to observe and critique the musicality of the content. Indicate the results on the assessment chart. (See TOPICS TO ASSESS FOR MUSICALITY.)

- Listen again to observe and critique the musicality of the execution. Indicate the results on the assessment chart. (See TOPICS TO ASSESS FOR MUSICALITY.)

- Listen again to observe and critique the quality of your instrumental technique. Indicate the results on the assessment chart. (See TOPICS TO ASSESS FOR MUSICALITY.)

- Refer to the TOPICS TO ASSESS FOR MUSICALITY list and indicate the strengths and/or weaknesses in your improvising *by number* under TOPIC #s on the ASSESSMENT CHART.

- If your improvising was satisfactory in all areas regarding the accuracy and musicality, your Stage of Musical Development equals the level of the musical context you selected. Enter this under the words CURRENT RATING on the ASSESSMENT CHART.

Exercise 2

Practice observing and critiquing the accuracy and musicality of live jazz performances as well as the recorded and transcribed improvised solos of accomplished jazz players. Begin with the recorded solos which are the most familiar to you. Use the TOPICS TO ASSESS FOR MUSICALITY list as a guide.

14. Private Practice, Jam Sessions and Jazz Gigs: A Balancing Act

Any event, experience or activity in which you participate that involves the making or studying of music can be considered musical practice, the three main ones for jazz players being: private practice sessions, jam sessions and jazz gigs.

I recommend that you take as much control as possible over the more controllable areas of your learning experience, such as private practice sessions and jam sessions. Jazz gigs are much less controllable, in the sense that you just can't expect to play a jazz gig whenever you want – unless you happen to be a bass player. Or a night club owner. Or a trombone player who doubles on bass *and* owns a night club!

Engaging in a flexible balance of these three activities (private practice sessions, jam sessions and jazz gigs) is necessary for you to evolve as a jazz improviser because:

- **Private Practice Sessions** – are where you

    acquire and refine specific musical strengths by adjusting the exercises and practice settings to fit your level of ability,

    learn how to *listen first, play second* while you improvise with play-along recordings,

    record, discover and critique your musical strengths and weaknesses without being distracted or intimidated by other players and listeners,

    build a repertoire and develop material to use in your improvising,

    prepare yourself to play jam sessions; and

- **Jam Sessions** – are where you

    use the strengths acquired from private practice sessions (such as *listen first, play second* while you improvise) to create and explore music with other players (i.e., your peers) who confirm your development and from whom you get ideas and inspiration,

    try out and test (and record and critique) the musical discoveries you make in private practice sessions,

    find out what works and what doesn't work in a group setting on the bandstand,

    build a network of peers and discover the potential a group of players may have to form a working band,

    prepare yourself to play jazz gigs; and

- **Jazz Gigs, Concerts, etc.** – are where you

    encounter the added pressure of paying customers, all of whom will be expecting you to *listen first, play second* while you improvise,

    try out and test (and record and critique) the musical discoveries you make at jam sessions,

    find out what works and what doesn't work in a group setting on the bandstand before a live audience,

    build a professional reputation and discover the potential a working band may have to tour and record, and

    prepare yourself to perform nightly at world-renowned jazz venues in places like New York City – or, decide you might be better off getting a degree and teaching public school in Vermont.

During certain periods of time, such as from the beginning of January to the end of November of each year, you may do more private practicing and jam sessions and far fewer jazz gigs. During other periods, such as from the end of November to the beginning of January of each year, you may do fewer jazz gigs and far more practicing and jam sessions! Good luck with this one.

But whether you schedule a jam session instead of your regular private practicing two or three times a week, or just add several jam sessions a week to your current private practice schedule, combining this with one or two jazz gigs per week (or per month, or per year!) will be extremely beneficial to your growth and development as a jazz improviser. And don't ask yourself if you can afford to spend time playing jam sessions in addition to, or instead of, your regular private practice; ask yourself if you can afford *not* to – especially if you're a trombone player who doesn't double on bass *or* own a night club!

Important

If you are a beginner or intermediate-level improviser and rarely (or never) get the opportunity to play with players that are more experienced and evolved than you are, I recommend that you hire some advanced-level players to play sessions and/or perform with you occasionally. This practice may be ridiculed and rejected by some people (hopefully not by the players you try to hire), but it is entirely respectable behavior as long as you think of it as a private lesson and remember not to equate your own level of musicianship with that of the better players you pay to play with you. It is better to measure your musical ability not by who *you* call (and pay) to play, but instead by who calls (and pays) you. And, if you are serious about improving, don't wait for players to call you to play a jam session; *you* should take the initiative and call them.

Since it's very important to learn how to function musically with partial rhythm section accompaniment as well as with full accompaniment, include duo and trio jam sessions in your session schedule. Remember: The more players there are in the band, the less time there will be for each player to solo. This is an important consideration, because the quantity of soloing time and experience you get at each jam session will directly effect the quality you are able to produce, especially if you are a beginner or intermediate-level improviser. Plus, it is much more convenient and practical to schedule several duo and trio sessions per week than larger size bands.

Exercises

• Schedule 15 to 20 duo, trio and quartet jam sessions per week (and at least twice as many during the holiday season), because with this amount of scheduled sessions per week you may end up actually playing once or twice. Control these sessions so that you are certain to get the musical benefit you need from them by selecting the material to play and choosing the keys and tempos in which to play it.

Whereas advanced-level players may be able to improve somewhat when playing with weaker players once in a while, beginner and intermediate-level players almost certainly will not. Therefore, try to select players who are at the same level of musical development as you or higher.

• (CD 1 and/or 2)

Schedule soloing sessions in which you and one other melodic instrument player practices soloing with play-along recordings versus live accompaniment. Solo separately at first, then include soloing simultaneously, or soloing by trading choruses, or by trading sections of the song's form, or by trading four-measure phrases, etc.

• Record and critique your practice daily.

15. Designing a Personal Practice Routine

Six Major Practice Areas

When designing your own daily practice routine, consider the six fundamentally important areas of musical training explained below. Include some or all of these areas in your daily practice. (For an example, see ahead to THE BASIC DESIGN, page 78.)

I. Instrumental Technique

Select or create exercises suitable to your level of development in the following subjects: warm-ups, scale and arpeggio patterns in major and minor keys, sound quality, intonation, articulation, dynamics, flexibility, range, register development, method book material, solo transcriptions, unique aspects of particular instruments.

II. Etudes

Select appropriate classical works/studies written for your instrument, designed to develop performance abilities related to execution, technique, expression and interpretation.

III. Sight Reading

Select different written material every day that is suitable to your level of development which features: jazz rhythm training (with and without pitch) incorporating swing feel and syncopation; pitch sequence training (with and without rhythm) incorporating key signatures as well as accidentals; vocabulary training; solo transcriptions; phrasing; various aspects of execution, etc. (See written musical examples throughout this text.)

IV. Repertoire

Select appropriate standard songs and standard jazz songs (see A. TUNE FILE, extra help, page 2). First learn the song's melody without the rhythm (i.e., the pitch sequence only); then learn the song's rhythm without the melody or pitch sequence (i.e., using a single note); then practice the song's melody and rhythm together; then learn the song's harmony (i.e., chord sequence) using root position arpeggios – first with equal duration on each chord, then with the song's actual harmonic rhythm. Learn one or two songs per week for several weeks, then review all previously learned songs for one week, etc. (See 4. REPERTOIRE AND EMBELLISHMENT, book I, page 79; also see HOW TO IMPROVISE: MEMORIZATION PROCEDURE, pages 23 and 24.)

V. Ear Training

For information see 3. EAR TRAINING, book I, page 73, and 6. CONTENT, book I, page 111.

VI. Improvisation

Select one or more topics of improvisation suitable to your level of development from the list below. Design appropriate exercises for each topic by selecting suitable restrictions. Practice the exercises in various musical contexts (i.e., with manageable harmonic settings, tempos, and modes of accompaniment). (See upcoming IMPROVISATION PRACTICE ROUTINE, page 79.)

Topics of Improvisation (Select topics to practice from this list.)

Pacing
Phrase Lengths
Rhythmic Density
Melodic and Rhythmic Embellishment of Song Melody
Guide-Tone Lines
Embellishing Guide-Tone Lines
Rhythmic Feel (Upbeat Placement)
Dynamics
Accents/Ghost Notes
Articulation
Syncopation
Rhythm Values
Vocabulary (Melodic/Rhythmic)
Chord-Tone Soloing
Lower Structure Triads
Chord-Scale Soloing
Nonharmonic Melody Notes
Upper Structure Triads

(Refer to HOW TO IMPROVISE and HOW TO COMP for additional information on many of the above topics.)

The Basic Design

During the course of a one year period, you could, for example, decide to practice the six major areas listed above as follows.

Three months focusing on:

• technique, improvisation, *etudes and sight-reading.*

Three months focusing on:

• technique, improvisation, *sight-reading and repertoire.*

Three months focusing on:

• technique, improvisation, *repertoire and ear training.*

Three months focusing on:

• technique, improvisation, *ear training and etudes.*

The above design is especially effective because it focuses on technique and improvisation (generally considered to be the two most important areas) for the entire 12 months of the year, and on the remaining areas for six months each using an overlapping system. (See DAILY PRACTICE ROUTINES on page 81 for suggested time allotments for each practice area. See end of this section for exercise.)

Improvisation Practice Routine: Selecting and Organizing Materials

To organize a daily practice routine specifically for improvisation, make selections with the help of a private teacher from the following six categories based on

- your general or overall level of ability (or STAGE OF MUSICAL DEVELOPMENT) as an instrumentalist and as an improviser, and

- the total amount of time you can realistically commit daily to practicing improvisation. (See ahead to DAILY PRACTICE ROUTINES for suggestions about allocating practice time to the six major areas of study. Also see EXAMPLE PLAN, page 84.)

I. Topics

Select one or more topics of improvisation (see previous list) suitable to your stage of musical development to practice individually and/or in combination with other topics.

II. Exercises

Design appropriate exercise instructions (i.e., restrictions) to provide a target for your improvising and to help you explore the selected topic in different ways. For example, one exercise for the topic *pacing* could be: Throughout the solo, play short phrases (two to eight beats in length), rest four to eight beats in between. Another exercise for *pacing* could be: Throughout the solo, play long phrases (four to six measures in length), rest three to four measures in between, etc.

One to several exercises can be created for each topic you select to practice. Or, you can select only one topic to practice, design a single exercise for that topic, and then practice this same exercise in different harmonic settings, at different tempos and with different modes of accompaniment, thereby creating numerous variations of the original exercise. (See DESIGNING EXERCISES FOR IMPROVISATION PRACTICE, pages 87-90.)

III. Harmonic Settings

Select one or more appropriate* harmonic settings in which to practice the selected topic(s), *beginning with the one that enables you to achieve maximum success (i.e., accuracy and musicality) with the topic.* Then include less familiar harmonic settings, or those which make accurate and musical execution of the selected topic, exercise, tempo and mode of accompaniment more challenging.

Choose from the following harmonic settings:

- **A single note** (played without harmonic accompaniment or played over a tune progression). (See 9. RESTRICT MELODY, EXPAND RHYTHM, page 31; and also B. PLAY-ALONG CDs 1 and 2, extra help, page 6.)

- **A single chord** (modal style). (See 9. RESTRICT HARMONY, EXPAND MELODY AND RHYTHM, page 31; and also B. PLAY-ALONG CD 1, extra help, page 6.)

- **A chord pattern** (V7 I, II–7 V7, II–7 V7 I, etc.) or any two-chord, three-chord or four-chord grouping isolated from a song's chord progression, with and without expanded chord durations. (See 2. HARMONY, CHORD PATTERNS, book I, page 52; and also B. PLAY-ALONG CD 1 and 2, extra help, page 6.)

- **A tune progression** (the chords of a song in the original key or transposed to other keys). (See B. PLAY-ALONG CD 2, extra help, page 15.)

- **"Free" harmony** (no harmonic restriction).

* **Note:** Certain combinations of topics and harmonic settings may be unsuitable, such as pentatonic scales with a single note, etc.

IV. Tempos

Select one or more appropriate* tempos at which to practice the selected topic(s) and harmonic setting(s), *beginning with the tempo that enables you to achieve maximum success (i.e., accuracy and musicality) with the material.* Then include less familiar tempos, or those which make accurate and musical execution of the selected topic, exercise, harmonic setting and mode of accompaniment more challenging.

Choose from the following tempo categories:

- **Medium** (comfortable, easy).
- **Slow** (as slow as you can play while accurately executing the topic and harmonic setting).
- **Fast** (as fast as you can play while accurately executing the topic and harmonic setting).
- **"Free" tempo or rubato** (without a steady tempo).
  - * **Note:** Certain combinations of topics and tempos may be unsuitable, such as rhythmic time-feel with rubato, etc.

V. Accompaniment

Select one or more appropriate* modes of accompaniment with which to practice the selected topic(s), harmonic setting(s) and tempo(s), *beginning with the one that enables you to achieve maximum success (i.e., accuracy and musicality) with the material.* Then include less familiar modes of accompaniment, or those which make accurate and musical execution of the selected topic, exercise, harmonic setting and tempo more challenging.

Choose from the following modes of accompaniment:

- **Full rhythm section**, i.e., piano (or guitar), bass and drums – with play-along recordings or live players. (See B. PLAY-ALONG CDs, extra help, page 6.)
- **Partial rhythm section**, i.e., piano and drums only, bass and drums only, piano and bass only, piano only, bass only, drums only – with play-along recordings or live players.
- **Metronome** (set metronome to click on all downbeats, or only on downbeats 2 and 4 at slow to medium-fast tempos in 4/4 time, and only on downbeats 1 and 3 at very fast tempos in 4/4 time).
- **A cappella** (no accompaniment).
  - * **Note:** Certain combinations of topics and modes of accompaniment may be unsuitable, such as upper structure triads with *a cappella*, etc.

VI. Solo Lengths

Set appropriate lengths for your practice solos with selected topics by considering the difficulty of the topic and exercise combined with the harmonic setting, tempo, and mode of accompaniment. Begin by playing and recording short solos (one minute, or one chorus in length) and then critiquing the recording of your improvising for accuracy in each of the previously mentioned areas. (See 13. SELF-CRITIQUING, page 58.)

Once the accuracy (technical correctness) of your improvising has been confirmed in the basic areas of tempo agreement (time), chord agreement (changes) and the exercise restrictions, set the solo length for five or more continuous minutes with each exercise. Your improvising with a particular topic and exercise must be accurate in a certain musical context first, then a substantial *quantity* of soloing experience (i.e., playing *long* solos on a daily basis) with this topic/exercise and in this context is necessary to produce quality, especially with beginner and intermediate level improvisers. (See end of this section for exercises.)

Daily Practice Routines

The following scenarios match-up various STAGES OF MUSICAL DEVELOPMENT (see page 66) with appropriate daily practice routines using 60, 90 and 120 minute practice periods. The content of these practice routines is based on the materials outlined in the SIX MAJOR PRACTICE AREAS (see page 77) and the IMPROVISATION PRACTICE ROUTINE (see page 79).

Consider these scenarios when designing your own practice routines, adjusting them wherever necessary to fit your personal situation.

Beginner Instrumentalist (Beginner Improviser)

Beginning, Intermediate and Advanced Sublevels.

- Daily Practice Time: 60 minutes (1 Hour).
   Instrumental Technique: 30 minutes.
   Etudes: 10 minutes.
   Sight-Reading: 10 minutes.
   Repertoire: 10 minutes.
   Ear Training: 0 minutes.
   Improvisation: 0 minutes.

   Note: Refer to the SIX BASIC PRACTICE AREAS, page 77, for the general content and instructions regarding each practice area listed above.

- Daily Practice Time: 90 minutes (1 and 1/2 Hours).
   Instrumental Technique; 45 (or 30) minutes.
   Etudes: 15 (or 10) minutes.
   Sight-Reading: 15 (or 10) minutes.
   Repertoire: 15 (or 10) minutes.
   Ear Training: 0 (or 10) minutes.
   Improvisation: 0 (or 20) minutes.

- Daily Practice Time: 120 minutes (2 Hours).
   Instrumental Technique: 60 (or 45) minutes.
   Etudes: 20 (or 10) minutes.
   Sight-Reading: 20 (or 10) minutes.
   Repertoire: 20 (or 10) minutes.
   Ear Training: 0 (or 15) minutes.
   Improvisation: 0 (or 30) minutes.

Intermediate Instrumentalist (Beginner or Intermediate Improviser)

Beginning, Intermediate and Advanced Sublevels.

- Daily Practice Time: 60 minutes.
   Instrumental Technique: 20 minutes.
   Etudes: 0 minutes/optional.
   Sight-Reading: 0 minutes/optional.
   Repertoire: 20 (or 10) minutes.
   Ear Training: 0 minutes/optional.
   Improvisation: 20 (or 30) minutes.

- Daily Practice Time: 90 minutes.
  Instrumental Technique: 30 minutes.
  Etudes: 0 minutes/optional.
  Sight-Reading: 0 minutes/optional.
  Repertoire: 30 (or 15) minutes.
  Ear Training: 0 (or 15) minutes.
  Improvisation: 30 minutes.

- Daily Practice Time: 120 minutes.
  Instrumental Technique: 40 minutes.
  Etudes: 0 minutes/optional.
  Sight-Reading: 0 minutes/optional.
  Repertoire: 40 (or 20) minutes.
  Ear Training: 0 (or 20) minutes.
  Improvisation: 40 minutes.

Advanced Instrumentalist (Beginner or Intermediate Improviser)

Beginning, Intermediate and Advanced Sublevels.

Note: You can also use the above plans for Intermediate Instrumentalist (Beginner or Intermediate Improviser) here but with more challenging material and settings.

- Daily Practice Time: 60 minutes.
  Instrumental Technique: 15 minutes.
  Repertoire: 10 (or 0) minutes.
  Ear Training: 0 (or 10) minutes.
  Improvisation: 35 minutes.

- Daily Practice Time: 90 minutes.
  Instrumental Technique: 20 minutes.
  Repertoire: 10 (or 0) minutes.
  Ear Training: 0 (or 10) minutes.
  Improvisation: 60 minutes.

- Daily Practice Time: 120 minutes.
  Instrumental Technique: 30 minutes.
  Repertoire: 15 (or 0) minutes.
  Ear Training: 15 (or 30) minutes.
  Improvisation: 60 minutes.

Advanced Instrumentalist (Advanced Improviser)

Beginning, Intermediate and Advanced Sublevels.

Note: You can also use the above plans for Advanced Instrumentalist (Beginner or Intermediate Improviser) here but with more challenging improvising material.

- Daily Practice Time: 60 minutes.
  Instrumental Technique: 15 (or 20) minutes.
  Ear Training: 0 (or 20) minutes.
  Improvisation: 45 (or 20) minutes.

- Daily Practice Time: 90 minutes.
  Instrumental Technique: 15 (or 30) minutes.
  Ear Training: 15 (or 30) minutes.
  Improvisation: 60 (or 30) minutes.

- Daily Practice Time: 120 minutes.
  Instrumental Technique: 30 minutes.
  Ear Training: 30 (or 60) minutes.
  Improvisation: 60 (or 30) minutes.

Exercise

Either by yourself or with a teacher's help, use the following EXAMPLE PLAN in conjunction with the information presented in the STAGES OF MUSICAL DEVELOPMENT (page 64), the SIX MAJOR PRACTICE AREAS (page 77), the IMPROVISATION PRACTICE ROUTINE (page 79), and the DAILY PRACTICE ROUTINES (page 81) to design a written daily practice schedule for yourself. Be sure to select topics, exercises and practice settings which are suitable to your level of musical development (i.e., challenging but playable).

Important

The following EXAMPLE PLAN is presented as a model for your daily practice routine. This plan is a three-page sample form which can be photocopied multiple times for your day to day use. Several examples showing how the plan can be used immediately follow the three-page Example Plan.

Example Plan for Daily Practice Routines

Six Major Practice Areas

Fill in the date and check off the areas you have selected for daily practice each time you restructure your practice routine (e.g., once every two or three months).

Dates									
Technique									
Etudes									
Sight Reading									
Repertoire									
Ear Training									
Improvisation									

Practice Materials and Time Allotments

List the exercises and materials you have selected to practice for technique, etudes, sight-reading, repertoire and/or ear training. (See SIX MAJOR PRACTICE AREAS, page 77.) Assign time allotments for each practice area depending on your Stage of Musical Development and time availability. (See DAILY PRACTICE ROUTINES, page 81.)

_____

_____

_____

_____

_____

_____

_____

_____

_____

_____

_____

_____

_____

_____

_____

_____

_____

_____

Example Plan, page 1

● Record and critique your practice daily.

Improvisation Practice Routine (Topics, Exercises and Settings)

(For examples see DESIGNING EXERCISES FOR IMPROVISATION PRACTICE, page 87.)

Topic (and date): _____

Time Allotment: 10 or more minutes per day

Exercise: create restrictions that help you explore the topic

Harmonic Setting: select from list on page 84

Tempo: select from list on page 84

Accompaniment: select from list on page 84

Solo Lengths: short (at first) to check for accuracy, then long to develop musicality

Topic (and date): _____

Time Allotment: _____

Exercise: _____

Harmonic Setting: _____

Tempo: _____

Accompaniment: _____

Topic (and date): _____

Time Allotment: _____

Exercise: _____

Harmonic Setting: _____

Tempo: _____

Accompaniment: _____

Topic (and date): _____

Time Allotment: _____

Exercise: _____

Harmonic Setting: _____

Tempo: _____

Accompaniment: _____

Example Plan, page 2

• Record and critique your practice daily.

(to photocopy)

Weekly Jam Session Schedule

1) Duo (day, date, time, place, personnel, instrumentation, telephone):

_____

_____

2) Duo (day, date, time, place, personnel, instrumentation, telephone):

_____

_____

3) Duo (day, date, time, place, personnel, instrumentation, telephone):

_____

_____

_____

1) Trio (day, date, time, place, personnel, instrumentation, telephone):

_____

_____

2) Trio (day, date, time, place, personnel, instrumentation, telephone):

_____

_____

3) Trio (day, date, time, place, personnel, instrumentation, telephone):

_____

_____

_____

1) Quartet (day, date, time, place, personnel, instrumentation, telephone):

_____

_____

2) Quartet (day, date, time, place, personnel, instrumentation, telephone):

_____

_____

3) Quartet (day, date, time, place, personnel, instrumentation, telephone):

_____

_____

_____

• Record and critique your practice daily

Example Plan, page 3

(to photocopy)

Designing Exercises for Improvisation Practice

Following are ten examples relating to the material on *improvisation* in the previous PLAN FOR DAILY PRACTICE ROUTINES outline beginning on page 84. The exercises may be considered separately or viewed all together as a complete two-hour practice routine. Also, see beyond EXAMPLE 10 below for variations.

Examples

1)

Topic (and date):	Pacing (i.e., controlling the duration of playing and resting throughout the solo)
Time Allotment:	15 minutes
Exercise:	Play 4 to 8 beats, rest 4 to 8 beats (throughout the solo)
Harmonic Setting:	Single-note solo (i.e., rhythm only)
Tempo:	♩ = 80 (for 5 min.), 100 (for 5 min.), and 120 (for 5 min.)
Accompaniment:	Metronome only, on beats 1, 2, 3 and 4

2)

Topic (and date):	Pacing
Time Allotment:	15 minutes
Exercise:	Play 4 to 8 beats, rest 4 to 8 beats (throughout the solo)
Harmonic Setting:	Single chords (i.e., modal style) selected from a chosen tune progression, using chord tones only (root, 3rd, 5th and 7th)
Tempo:	♩ = 80 (for 5 min.), 100 (for 5 min.), and 120 (for 5 min.)
Accompaniment:	Metronome only, on beats 1, 2, 3 and 4

3)

Topic (and date):	Pacing
Time Allotment:	15 minutes
Exercise:	Play 4 to 8 beats, rest 4 to 8 beats (throughout the solo)
Harmonic Setting:	2-chord and 3-chord groupings selected from the chosen tune progression, with or without expanded chord durations, using chord tones only
Tempo:	♩ = 80 (for 5 min.), 100 (for 5 min.), and 120 (for 5 min.)
Accompaniment:	Metronome only, on beats 2 and 4, then on beats 1 and 3

4)

Topic (and date):	Pacing
Time Allotment:	15 minutes
Exercise:	Play 4 to 8 beats, rest 4 to 8 beats (throughout the solo)
Harmonic Setting:	Use complete tune progression, first with equal duration on each chord, then with actual duration on each chord, using chord tones only
Tempo:	♩ = 80 (for 5 min.), 100 (for 5 min.), and 120 (for 5 min.)
Accompaniment:	Metronome only, on beats 2 and 4, then on beats 1 and 3

5)

Topic (and date):	Chord-tone soloing (i.e. using the root, 3rd, 5th and 7th only on each chord)
Time Allotment:	10 minutes
Exercise:	Use chord tones only and a *different* rhythm motive for each individual chord, play 1 to several measures then rest 1 measure (if necessary) throughout the solo *
Harmonic Setting:	Select 5 individual chords from a chosen tune progression, play for 2 minutes on each chord (i.e., modal style)
Tempo:	♩ = 120
Accompaniment:	None

* see pages 28-29 for rhythm motives

6)

Topic (and date):	Chord-tone soloing
Time Allotment:	10 minutes
Exercise:	Use chord tones only and a *different* rhythm motive for each chord, play 1 to several measures then rest 1 measure (if necessary) throughout the solo, feature wide melodic intervals (e.g., 7ths, 8ths, 9ths, 10ths, 11ths, 12ths, etc.)
Harmonic Setting:	Select the same 5 individual chords (or different ones) from the chosen tune progression, play for 2 minutes on each chord (i.e., modal style)
Tempo:	♩ = 60
Accompaniment:	None

7)

Topic (and date):	Chord-tone soloing
Time Allotment:	10 minutes
Exercise:	Use chord tones only and a *different* rhythm motive for each chord, play 1 to several measures then rest 1 measure (if necessary) throughout the solo, feature melodic repeated notes (2 to 6 attacks)
Harmonic Setting:	Select the same 5 individual chords (or different ones) from the chosen tune progression, play for 2 minutes on each chord (i.e., modal style)
Tempo:	♩ = 140
Accompaniment:	Metronome only, on beats 2 and 4, then on beats 1 and 3

8)

Topic (and date):	Chord-tone soloing
Time Allotment:	10 minutes
Exercise:	Use chord tones only and a different rhythm motive for each chord, play/rest, feature wide melodic intervals and melodic repeated notes
Harmonic Setting:	Select the same 5 individual chords (or different ones) from the chosen tune progression, play for 2 minutes on each chord (i.e., modal style)
Tempo:	♩ = 92
Accompaniment:	Pre-recorded bass line (or root motion line) with metronome

9)

Topic (and date):	Chord-tone soloing
Time Allotment:	10 minutes
Exercise:	Use chord tones only and *improvise the melodic rhythm* (instead of using rhythm motives), play/rest
Harmonic Setting:	Select the same 5 individual chords (or different ones) from the chosen tune progression, play for 2 minutes on each chord (i.e., modal style)
Tempo:	♩ = 120
Accompaniment:	Drums only

10)

Topic (and date):	Chord-tone soloing
Time Allotment:	10 minutes
Exercise:	Use chord tones only and rhythm motives (then improvise the melodic rhythm), play/rest, feature wide melodic intervals and melodic repeated notes
Harmonic Setting:	Use the complete tune progression, first with equal duration on each chord, then with actual duration on each chord
Tempo:	♩ = 112
Accompaniment:	Full rhythm section (i.e., play along recording)

Variations on the above Examples

- With examples 1 through 4 of exercises on pacing above, change content of EXERCISE to "play 2 to 3 measures, rest 2 to 3 measures." Then at faster tempos use "play 2 to 3 measures, rest 4 to 6 measures." Also, combine various pacing restrictions with restrictions of execution, such as articulation patterns, accents and ghost notes, exaggerated natural dynamics, etc.

- With examples #5 through 10 of exercises on chord-tone soloing above, change content of HARMONIC SETTING to "two-chord groupings from selected tune progression." Adjust tempos and accompaniment accordingly. Also, change TOPIC to "Chord-Scale Soloing" and repeat all exercises.

APPENDIX

About the Author

Please visit www.halcrook.com for more information than you will ever need or want to know about Hal Crook.

Hal Crook's Selected Discography

Phil Woods
ALL BIRD'S CHILDREN, Concord Jazz
FULL HOUSE, Milestone (NY)
EVOLUTION, Concord Jazz
REAL LIFE, Chesky Records (NY)
FLASH, Concord Jazz (CA)
20TH ANNIVERSARY SET, Mosaic (NY)
INTO THE WOODS, Concord Jazz
CELEBRATION (nominated for Grammy Award, 1998), Concord Jazz

Jerry Bergonzi/Hal Crook
CONJUNCTION, Konnex Records (Germany)

Clark Terry
JUST FRIENDS, UNH Records (NH)

Joe Diorio/Hal Crook
NARAYANI, with Steve LaSpina and Steve Bagby, RAM Records (Italy)

Daniel Humair
QUATRE FOIS TROIS, with George Garzone, Label Bleu (France)

Der Rote Bereich
DER ROTE BEREICH 2, with Frank Mobus, Rudi Mahall and Jim Black, Jazz4Ever (Germany)

Hal Crook
GIZMOSIS, with John Medeski, Rope-A-Dope Records, NYC
HERO WORSHIP, with Paul Motian and Mick Goodrick, RAM Records (Italy)
ONLY HUMAN, with Bob Gullotti and John Lockwood, RAM Records
TRIO I, II AND III, with Dave Weigert, Outland Music
HELLO HEAVEN, with Phil Woods, Bill Dobbins, Chuck Israels and Bill Goodwin, Omnisound Jazz
CREATIVE COMPING FOR IMPROVISATION, VOL. I, II, III, Advance Music

Hal Crook plays a King 3B tenor trombone with a Bach 7C mouthpiece.

Reviews

"Trombonist Hal Crook is a marvel. [He] has evolved a singular musical voice echoing past masters ... impressing as a modernist with chops."
Jazz Times

"In replacing Tom Harrell, Phil Woods could hardly have made a better choice than trombonist Hal Crook. Crook plays with Swiss-movement precision but without sacrificing emotion as he detonates chorus after agile chorus. A prominent soloist of this caliber can do much to restore the trombone as a popular small-band voice."
Los Angeles Times

"A model of musicality ... Crook blows with fluent urgency or considered lyricism and never scrimps on content ... He is also a superior composer."
Boston Globe

"Crook's playing reflects both the traditional and the modern. He has exceptional control of the trombone, playing with an even tone and precise intonation throughout the instrument's range. A superb ballad player, a gifted composer and arranger ... [He] has all the tools to be a major voice on the trombone."
Down Beat

"Hal Crook's elegant trombone style, his singing tone and fluid execution, showers the listener with waves of sound: music of the highest order."
Stereophile

"The sweet, deep and steady tone of Crook's trombone takes the group (Phil Woods Quintet) into another dimension, adding fullness ... As a soloist, Crook tames the often unruly trombone so that the sound is fluid and lush, but with a modern feel."
Seattle Post

"Hal Crook, a superb soloist, can make the trombone do anything he wants, and yet not sound finicky or smug about it."
Down Beat

"Hal Crook, the young trombone virtuoso, darkens the band's (PWQ) voice ... but also makes his instrument dance high in the trumpet's register."
New York Magazine

"Crook is a trombonist who combines the slide features of the instrument with the trip-hammer articulation of bop. He's very impressive."
Down Beat

"Hal Crook is an astonishing player – there's no other word for it."
Cadence